STAR PEOPLE, SKY GODS
AND OTHER
TALES OF THE NATIVE
AMERICAN INDIANS

WRITTEN AND EDITED BY G.W. MULLINS

WITH ORIGINAL ART BY C.L. HAUSE

LIGHT
OF THE
MOON
PUBLISHING

ISBN: 978-1-64008-093-5

First Edition Printing

Light Of The Moon Publishing has allowed this work to remain exactly as the author intended, verbatim, without editorial input.

Printed in the United States of America

The following book represents a collection of Native American works which are public domain. You may have read the stories before. In true story telling fashion, the stories have been left as close to the original form as possible. In Native American culture, in order to pass the stories along with all information intact, they had to be told pretty much word for word, to keep the legends alive. Many of these stories were translated directly from original Native language texts. With that in mind, please be aware that some spellings and word usage may vary from one tribe to another. For instance, the spelling of "teepee", as used in this book, can also be written as "tipi", and "tepee". All are correct. Also when using words like "someone", in most native cultures, it would be "some one". So keep in mind, these are not necessarily misspellings. They are simply dialect and translations.

This book is dedicated to Vince Mullins, my Grandfather (Pawpaw). He was a tall red man with fire in his eyes... who I loved so much.

G.W. Mullins

This book is also dedicated to Chief Dan George, a true visionary.

**"May the stars carry your sadness away,
May the flowers fill your heart with beauty,
May hope forever wipe away your tears,
And, above all, may silence make you strong."
~ Chief Dan George**

Chief Dan George, (July 24, 1899 – September 23, 1981) was a chief of the Tsleil-Waututh Nation, a Coast Salish band located on Burrard Inlet in North Vancouver, British Columbia, Canada. He was also an author, poet, actor, and an Officer of the Order of Canada. At the age of 71, he was nominated for an Academy Award for Best Supporting Actor in Little Big Man.

Also Available From G.W. Mullins And C.L. Hause

Walking With Spirits Native American Myths, Legends, And Folklore
Volumes One Thru Six

The Native American Cookbook

Native American Cooking - An Indian Cookbook With Legends And Folklore

The Native American Story Book - Stories Of The American Indians For Children
Volumes One Thru Five

The Best Native American Stories For Children

Cherokee A Collection of American Indian Legends, Stories And Fables

Creation Myths - Tales Of The Native American Indians

Strange Tales Of The Native American Indians

Spirit Quest - Stories Of The Native American Indians

Animal Tales Of The Native American Indians

Medicine Man - Shamanism, Natural Healing, Remedies And Stories Of The Native
American Indians

Native American Legends: Stories Of The Hopi Indians
Volumes One and Two

Totem Animals Of The Native Americans

The Best Native American Myths, Legends And Folklore
Volumes One Thru Three

Ghosts, Spirits And The Afterlife In Native American Indian Mythology And
Folklore

The Native American Art Book – Art Inspired By Native American Myths And
Legends

"The man who sat on the ground in his tipi meditating on life and its meaning, accepting the kinship of all creatures, and acknowledging unity with the universe of things, was infusing into his being the true essence of civilization."
--Luther Standing Bear, OGLALA SIOUX

Table of Contents

Introduction 11
The Story of Poïa 14
The Legend of Star Boy (Origin of the Sun-dance) 19
Star Maiden 23
Origin of the Sweat Lodge (A Second Story of Scarface) 29
How the Milky Way Came To Be 34
The Snake with the Big Feet 36
The Origin of the Pleiades and the Pine 41
Falling-Star 44
The Story of the Land of Northern Lights 51
The Hunting of the Great Bear 55
How the Great Chiefs Made the Moon and the Sun 62
Tale of Coyote Regulates Life After Death 66
They That Chase After the Bear 68
Tale of the Lazy Boys Who Became the Pleiades 71
The Sun Tests His Son-in-law 73
Tale of the Man and the Dog Who Became Stars 87
The Moon and the Thunders 89
Tale of Evening-Star and Orphan-Star 93
Tale of the Girl Who Had Power to Call the Buffalo 96
The Man Who Married the Moon 98
Tales of the Girl Who Married a Star 109
The Two War Gods and the Two Maidens 113
The Man in the Moon 115
Tale of the Girl Who Married a Star 2 117
Children of the Sun 121
The Woman Who Fell from the Sky 123
Sun Sister and Moon Brother 128
Why the North Star Stands Still 130
Eagle Boy 134
The Wish to Marry a Star 140
Old Man Above Creates the World 143
The Nunne'hi and Other Spirit Folk 145
The Spirit Defenders of Nikwasi' 155
Blood Clot Boy 159

The Story of Poïa
A Blackfoot Legend

Once during the summer in the earliest times, when it was too hot to sleep indoors, a beautiful maiden named Feather-woman slept outside in the tall prairie grass.

She opened her eyes just as the Morning Star came into view, and she began to look on it with wonder. She mused in her heart how beautiful it was, and she fell in love with it.

When her sisters got up, she told them that she had fallen in love with the Morning Star. They told her that she was insane! Feather-woman told everyone in her village about the Morning Star and soon she was an object of ridicule among her people.

One day she left the village to draw some water out of a creek. There she saw the most handsome young man she had ever imagined. At first she thought that he was a young man of her own tribe who had been hunting, and she coyly avoided him. But he then identified himself as the Morning Star.

He said, "I know that you were watching me and fell in love with me. Even as you were looking up at the sky, I was looking down at you. I watched you in the tall prairie grass and knew that it was only you that I wanted for my wife. Come with me to my home in the sky."

Feather-woman was stricken with awe and paralyzed with fear. She knew that this was a god standing before her. She told Morning Star that she would need time to say good-bye to her parents and sisters. However, he told her that there was no time for this.

He then gave her a magic yellow feather in one hand and a
juniper branch in the other. Then he told her to close her
eyes. When she opened them again, she was in the Sky-
Country, standing before the lodge of Morning Star, home
of his parents, the Sun and the Moon, where they were
married. As it was daytime, the Sun was out doing his
work, but the mother, the Moon, was at home doing chores.
She immediately took a liking to the girl and gave her fine
robes to wear.

Feather-woman loved her husband and his parents, and in
time she gave birth to a little boy whom they named Star
Boy. But Feather-woman needed to find things to do in her
new home. So the Moon gave her a root-digging stick to
work with, carefully instructing her not to dig up the Great
Turnip that grew near the home of the Spider Man, warning
that terrible ills would be unleashed if she did so.

Feather-woman was fascinated by the Great Turnip and
wondered why it was feared. After all, it looked like any
other turnip, only much larger. She walked closely around
it, being careful not to touch it. She took Star Boy off her
back and placed him on the ground. As she was digging,
two great cranes flew overhead. She asked the cranes to
help her and they obliged her, singing a secret magic song
that made light work of digging the Great Turnip.

Now, the Moon had been very wise in warning Feather-
woman not to dig around the Great Turnip, for it plugged
the hole through which Morning Star had brought Feather-
woman into the Sky-Country. With a loud plop she pulled
the Great Turnip out. Looking down through the hole, she
saw a camp of the Blackfoot Indians, perhaps her own
village, far below her.

As she saw the mortals doing their daily chores below, she became homesick and began to weep. In order to conceal what she had done, she rolled the turnip loosely into place and returned to the lodge where she lived with her husband and son.

When Morning Star returned to the lodge, he was very sad. He said nothing, then, "How could you have been disobedient and dug up the Great Turnip?" Moon and Sun were also sad and asked her the same question.

At first Feather-woman did not answer, then she admitted her disobedience. Her in-laws had known that she would dig up the Great Turnip, despite their warnings. The reason for the sadness was that they knew that she had disobeyed them and must now be banished forever from the Sky-Country.

The next day, Morning Star took his wife to Spider Man, who built a web from the hole of the Great Turnip down to earth. When Feather-woman descended down the web, it looked to the people below like a star falling from the sky.

When Feather-woman arrived on earth with her child, she was welcomed by her parents and the people of their village. But she was never happy. Early in the morning, she looked up at the sky to speak with Morning Star, but he didn't answer her.

After many months had passed, Morning Star finally did speak to her. "You can never return to the Sky-Country," he warned. "You committed a great sin and brought unhappiness and death into the world." Hearing this was too much for Feather-woman to bear; soon she died of her unhappiness.

The orphaned Star Boy lived with his human grandparents
until they died. He was a shy boy who ran as soon as he
heard the approach of a stranger's footsteps. The most
notable thing about him was a scar on his face, which led to
his nickname, Poïa, meaning "scar face." As he grew into
manhood, people cruelly ridiculed him because of his scar
and his pretension to be the son of the Morning star.

Thus maltreated, Poïa was heartbroken by the further
indignity of being rejected by the daughter of a chief. His
life growing unbearable, Poïa consulted with an old
medicine woman. She told him that there was only one way
for the scar to be removed: He would have to return to the
Sky-Country and have his grandfather, the Sun, take it off.

Knowing that his mother had been banished from the Sky-
Country, this was bad news to Poïa. How could he return to
the land of his birth? The old woman said that there was a
way back to the Sky-Country, but that Poïa must find it
himself. Feeling sorry for the boy, she gave him some food
for the journey.

Poïa traveled for days and days, over mountains, through
forests, through snow, and across deserts, until he reached
the Great Water that the white man calls the Pacific Ocean,
for this is the farthest west, where the sun goes at night. For
three days, Poïa fasted and prayed. On the third day, he saw
rays reflecting on the Great Water, forming a path to the
Sun. He followed the path and arrived at the home of his
grandparents, the Sun and the Moon.

Upon finding Poïa asleep on their doorstep, the Sun was at
first prepared to kill the mortal, as no earth-dweller could
enter the Sky-Country. But the Moon persuaded him not to
do so; she recognized the scar and told the Sun that it was
their grandson. Soon, Moon, Sun, and Morning Star all

welcomed Poïa. At the request of his grandson, the Sun removed the scar.

The Sun also taught Poïa great magic and the truths of the world. Poïa's grandfather explained that the people on earth were suffering as a result of Feather-woman's disobedience. The Sun had a message for the Blackfoot people: If they would honor him but once a year by doing the Sun dance, all the sick would be healed.

Poïa himself learned the Sun dance quickly, and his grandfather grew to love him very much. His grandparents gave him a magic flute to charm women into falling in love with him. But, because of his mother's disobedience, Poïa had to return to earth, which he did by walking down the Milky Way.

When Poïa returned to the Blackfoot people, they honored him. He taught them the wisdom he had learned from the Sun and, most important, he taught them how to do the Sun dance, which indeed healed the sick. Because of Poïa's great deeds, the Sun and Moon allowed him to bring his new wife, the chief's daughter who had once rejected him, to the Sky-Country, where they remained forever. Now Poïa himself is a star that rises with the Morning Star.

The Legend of Star Boy (Origin of the Sun-dance)

A Blackfoot Legend

We know not when the Sun-dance had its origin. It was long ago, when the Blackfeet used dogs for beasts of burden instead of horses; when they stretched the legs and bodies of their dogs on sticks to make them large, and when they used stones instead of wooden pegs to hold down their lodges. In those days, during the moon of flowers (early summer), our people were camped near the mountains. It was a cloudless night and a warm wind blew over the prairie. This was when the story of Poïa (Scarface) began.

When Poïa became a young man, he loved a maiden of his own tribe. She was very beautiful and the daughter of a leading chief. Many of the young men wanted to marry her, but she refused them all. Poïa sent this maiden a present, with the message that he wanted to marry her, but she was proud and disdained his love. She scornfully told him, she would not accept him as her lover, until he would remove the scar from his face. Scarface was deeply grieved by the reply. He consulted with an old medicine woman, his only friend. She revealed to him, that the scar had been placed on his face by the Sun God, and that only the Sun himself could remove it. Poïa resolved to go to the home of the Sun God. The medicine woman made moccasins for him and gave him a supply of pemmican.

Poïa journeyed alone across the plains and through the mountains, enduring many hardships and great dangers. Finally he came to the Big Water (Pacific Ocean). For three days and three nights he lay upon the shore, fasting and praying to the Sun God. On the evening of the fourth day, he beheld a bright trail leading across the water. He travelled this path until he grew near the home of the Sun, when he hid himself and waited.

In the morning, the great Sun Chief came from his lodge, ready for his daily journey. He did not recognize Poïa. Angered at beholding a creature from the earth, he said to the Moon, his wife, "I will kill him, for he comes from a good-for-nothing-race," but she interceded and saved his life. Morning Star, their only son, a young man with a handsome face and beautifully dressed, came forth from the lodge. He brought with him dried sweet grass, which he burned as incense. He first placed Poïa in the sacred smoke, and then led him into the presence of his father and mother, the Sun and the Moon. Poïa related the story of his long journey, because of his rejection by the girl he loved. Morning Star then saw how sad and worn he looked. He felt sorry for him and promised to help him.

Poïa lived in the lodge of the Sun and Moon with Morning Star. Once, when they were hunting together, Poïa killed seven enormous birds, which had threatened the life of Morning Star. He presented four of the dead birds to the Sun and three to the Moon. The Sun rejoiced, when he knew that the dangerous birds were killed, and the Moon felt so grateful, that she besought her husband to repay him. On the intercession of Morning Star, the Sun God consented to remove the scar. He also appointed Poïa as his messenger to the Blackfeet, promising, if they would give a festival (Sun-dance) in his honor, once every year, he would restore their sick to health. He taught Poïa the

secrets of the Sun-dance, and instructed him in the prayers
and songs to be used. He gave him two raven feathers to
wear as a sign that he came from the Sun, and a robe of
soft-tanned elk-skin, with the warning that it must be worn
only by a virtuous woman. She can then give the Sun-dance
and the sick will recover. Morning Star gave him a magic
flute and a wonderful song, with which he would be able to
charm the heart of the girl he loved.

Poïa returned to the earth and the Blackfeet camp by the
Wolf Trail (Milky Way), the short path to the earth. When
he had fully instructed his people concerning the Sun-
dance, the Sun God took him back to the sky with the girl
he loved. When Poïa returned to the home of the Sun, the
Sun God made him bright and beautiful, just like his father,
Morning Star. In those days Morning Star and his son could
be seen together in the east. Because Poïa appears first in
the sky, the Blackfeet often mistake him for his father, and
he is therefore sometimes called Poks-o-piks-o-aks,
Mistake Morning Star.

Morning Star was given to us as a sign to herald the coming
of the Sun. When he appears above the horizon, we know a
new day is about to dawn. Many medicine men have
dreamed of the Sun, and of the Moon, but have never yet
heard of one so powerful as to dream of Morning Star,
because he shows himself in the sky for such a short time.

The 'Star that stands still' (North Star) is different from
other stars, because it never moves. All the other stars walk
round it. It is a hole in the sky, the same hole through
which So-at-sa-ki was first drawn up to the sky and then let
down again to earth. It is the hole, through which she gazed
upon the earth, after digging up the forbidden turnip. Its
light is the radiance from the home of the Sun God shining
through. The half circle of stars to the east (Northern

Crown) is the lodge of the Spider Man, and the five bright stars just beyond (in the constellation of Hercules) are his Eve fingers, with which he spun the web, upon which So-at-sa-ki was let down from the sky. Whenever you see the half-buried and overgrown circles, or clusters of stones on the plains, marking the sites of Blackfeet camps in the ancient days, when they used stones to hold down the sides of their lodges, you will know why the half-circle of stars was called by our fathers, 'The Lodge of the Spider Man."

When So-at-sa-ki came back to earth from the lodge of the Sun, she brought with her the sacred Medicine Bonnet and dress trimmed with elk teeth, the Turnip Digger, Sweet Grass (incense), and the Prongs for lifting hot coals from the fire. Ever since those days, these sacred articles have been used in the Sun-dance by the woman who makes the vow. The Turnip Digger is always tied to the Medicine Case, containing the Medicine Bonnet, and it now hangs from the tripod behind my lodge.

Star Maiden

Waupee the White Hawk lived in a deep forest where animals and birds were abundant. Each day he returned from the chase well rewarded, for he was one of the most skillful hunters of his tribe. No part of the forest was too dark for him to penetrate, and there was no track he could not follow.

One day he went beyond any point he had visited before, through an open bit of forest which enabled him to see a great distance. Light breaking through showed that he was on the edge of a wide plain covered with grass. He walked here for some time without a path, then suddenly came to a ring worn down in the earth as if made by footsteps following a circle. What excited him was the fact that there was no path leading into the ring or away from it. He could find no trace of footsteps in any crushed leaf or broken twig.

Waupee thought he would hide and watch to see, if he could, what had made the circle. Very soon he heard faint sounds of music. He looked up and saw a small something descending to earth. From a mere speck it grew bigger and the music became stronger and sweeter. He beheld a basket in which rode twelve beautiful maidens.

As soon as the basket touched the ground, the girls leaped out. They began to dance round the magic ring, striking a shining ball as they flitted past. Waupee gazed upon their graceful movements. He admired them all, but most of all the youngest. Unable to restrain his admiration, suddenly he rushed out of his hiding place and tried to seize her. But the sisters, quick as birds, as soon as they saw him leaped into the basket and rose up into the sky.

Waupee gazed till he could see them no more. "They are gone, and I shall not see them again," he sighed. Filled with a deep sadness he returned to his lonely lodge. His mind could not rest. Hunting, his favorite sport, he could no longer enjoy, nor the companionship around the fire at night with the storytellers, nor the admiration of the girls of his tribe.

The next day Waupee returned to the prairie to wait near the ring. This time, in order to deceive the sisters, he assumed the form of an opossum. The basket again floated down, to the center of the magic ring, and once more he heard the sweet music. The maidens leaped out and began their sportive dancing. They seemed to Waupee to be even more beautiful and graceful this time.

In his disguise, Waupee crept slowly through the grass towards the ring, but the instant he appeared, ready to seize the youngest; the sisters sprang together into their basket. It rose, but when it was only a short distance off the ground, Waupee heard one of the older girls speak. "Perhaps," she said, "it came to show us how our game is played on earth."

"Oh, no!" replied the youngest, "Quick, let us ascend."

Once more the basket floated upward out of sight.

Waupee returned to his own form and walked sorrowfully back to his lodge. The night seemed long, and back to the plain he went early the next day. How could he secure that lovely maiden? While he pondered, he noticed an old stump of a tree near by in which mice were running about. He brought the stump over near the ring. "So small a creature would not cause alarm," he thought, and thereupon he turned himself into a mouse.

The sisters floated down and took up their game. "But, look," cried the youngest. "That stump was not there yesterday." Frightened, she ran to the basket. The others, however, only smiled and gathered around it. When they struck at it playfully, the mice ran out, Waupee among them. The girls killed all but one, which was pursued by the youngest sister. Just as she raised her stick to kill it, Waupee rose and clasped her in his arms. Her eleven sisters sprang quickly into their basket and rose up into the sky.

Waupee displayed all his skills, to please his bride and win her affection. As he wiped away her tears, he praised the way of life on earth. He was determined to make her forget her sisters. From the moment she entered his lodge with him, he was one of the happiest of men.

Winter and summer passed away and the girl found she loved this young hunter. Their happiness was greater when a beautiful boy was born to them.

But Waupee's wife was a daughter of one of the stars and she longed to visit her old home. While Waupee was hunting she managed to make a wicker basket, secretly, in the middle of the magic ring.

When it was finished she collected rarities, including special foods from earth, to please her father. With these she went one day when Waupee was away, taking her little son with her into the charmed ring. As soon as they had climbed into the basket, she began to sing and the basket rose.

The wind carried her song to her husband's ear. He recognized her voice and ran at once to the prairie. But he could not reach the ring before his wife and child were ascending. He called and called after them, but they did not heed his appeals. Waupee could only watch the basket until it was a small speck and finally vanished in the sky. In utter grief, he lay down on the ground.

Through a long winter and a long summer, Waupee bewailed his loss and could find no relief. He mourned for his wife and even more for his son.

In the meantime Waupee's wife had reached her home among the stars and almost forgot that she had left a husband on earth. The presence of her son reminded her, however, for as he grew up he began to wish to visit his father. One day his grandfather, who was the Star Chief, said to his daughter, "Go, take your son to see his father, and ask him to come to live with us. Tell him to bring with him one of each kind of bird and animal he kills in the chase."

Accordingly, Waupee's wife took the boy and descended to earth. Waupee, who was never far from the enchanted circle, heard her voice as she came down from the sky. His heart beat with impatience as he saw her and his son, and he soon had them in his arms.

His wife gave him her father's message and Waupee began
at once to hunt. Whole nights as well as days he searched
for every beautiful or curiously different bird and animal.
He took only a tail, foot, or wing--enough to identify each.
When all was ready, he went with his wife and child to the
circle and they floated up.

Great joy greeted their arrival in the starry world. The Star
Chief invited all his people to a feast. When they were
together, he announced that each might take one of the
earthly gifts, whichever was most admired. Some chose a
foot, some a wing, some a tail, and some a claw. Those
who selected a tail or claw became animals and ran off. The
others assumed the form of birds and flew away. Waupee
chose a white hawk's feather and his wife and son followed
his example. All three now became white hawks and spread
their great wings. They descended with the other birds
down to earth, where they may still be found.

Origin of the Sweat Lodge (A Second Story of Scarface)

The Piegan tribe was southernmost at the headwaters of the Missouri River in Montana, a sub-tribe belonging to the Siksika Indians of North Saskatchewan in Canada. Piegans were of the Algonquian linguistic family, but warlike toward most of their neighboring tribes, since they had horses for raiding and were supplied with guns and ammunition by their Canadian sources. Piegans also displayed hostility toward explorers and traders. Several smallpox epidemics decimated their population. Now they are gathered on reservations on both sides of the border.

A girl of great beauty, the Chief's daughter, was worshipped by many young handsome men of the Piegan tribe. But she would not have any one of them for her husband.

One young tribesman was very poor and his face was marked with an ugly scar. Although he saw rich and handsome men of his tribe rejected by the Chief's daughter, he decided to find out if she would have him for her husband. When she laughed at him for even asking, he ran away toward the south in shame.

After travelling several days, he dropped to the ground, weary and hungry, and fell asleep. From the heavens, Morning-Star looked down and pitied the young unfortunate youth, knowing his trouble.

To Sun and Moon, his parents, Morning-Star said, "There is a poor young man lying on the ground with no one to help him. I want to go after him for a companion."

"Go and get him," said his parents.

Morning-Star carried the young man, Scarface, into the sky. Sun said, "Do not bring him into my lodge yet, for he smells ill. Build four sweat lodges."

When this was done, Sun led Scarface into the first sweat lodge. He asked Morning-Star to bring a hot coal on a forked stick. Sun then broke off a bit of sweet grass and placed it upon the hot coal. As the incense arose Sun began to sing, "Old Man is coming in with his body; it is sacred," repeating it four times.

Sun passed his hands back and forth through the smoke and rubbed them over the face, left arm, and side of Scarface. Sun repeated the ceremony on the boy's right side, purifying him and removing the odors of earthly people.

Sun took Scarface into the other three sweat lodges, performing the same healing ceremony. The body of Scarface changed color and he shone like a yellow light.

Using a soft feather, Sun brushed it over the youth's face, magically wiping away the scar. With a final touch to the young man's long, yellow hair, Sun caused him to look exactly like Morning-Star. The two young men were led by Sun into his own lodge and placed side by side in the position of honor.

"Old Woman," called the father. "Which is your son?"

Moon pointed to Scarface, "That one is our son."

"You do not know your own child," answered Sun.

"He is not our son. We will call him Mistaken-for-Morning-Star," as they all laughed heartily at the mistake.

The two boys were together constantly and became close companions. One day, they were on an adventure when Morning-Star pointed out some large birds with very long, sharp beaks.

"Foster-Brother, I warn you not to go near those dangerous creatures," said Morning-Star. "They killed my other brothers with their beaks."

Suddenly the birds chased the two boys. Morning-Star fled toward his home, but Foster-Brother stopped, picking up a club and one by one struck the birds dead.

Upon reaching home, Morning-Star excitedly reported to his father what had happened. Sun made a victory song honoring the young hero. In gratitude for saving Morning-Star's life, Sun gave him the forked stick for lifting hot embers and a braid of sweet grass to make incense. These sacred elements necessary for making the sweat lodge ceremony were a gift of trust.

"And this my sweat lodge I give to you," said the Sun. Mistaken-for-Morning-Star observed very carefully how it was constructed, in his mind preparing himself to one day returning to earth.

When Scarface did arrive at his tribal village, all of his people gathered to see the handsome young man in their midst. At first, they did not recognize him as Scarface.

"I have been in the sky," he told them. "Behold me, Morning-Star looks just like this. The Sun gave me these things used in the sweat lodge healing ceremony. That is how I lost my ugly scar."

Scarface explained how the forked stick and sweet grass were used. Then he set to work showing his people how to make the sweat lodge. This is how the first medicine sweat lodge was built upon earth by the Piegan tribe.

Now that Scarface was so very handsome and brought such a great blessing of healing to his tribe, the Chief's beautiful daughter became his wife.

In remembrance of Sun's gift to Scarface and his tribe, the Piegans always make the sweat lodge healing ceremony an important part of their annual Sun Dance Celebration.

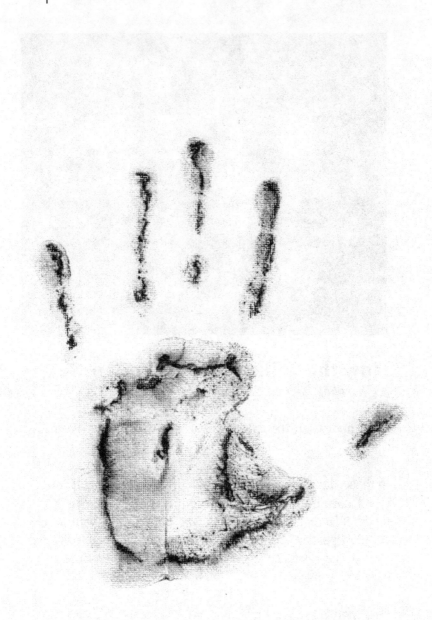

How the Milky Way Came To Be
A Cherokee Legend

Long ago when the world was young, there were not many stars in the sky.

In those days the people depended on corn for their food. Dried corn could be made into corn meal by placing it inside a large hollowed stump and pounding it with a long wooden pestle. The cornmeal was stored in large baskets. During the winter, the ground meal could be made into bread and mush.

One morning an old man and his wife went to their storage basket for some cornmeal. They discovered that someone or something had gotten into the cornmeal during the night. This upset them very much for no one in a Cherokee village stole from someone else.

Then they noticed that the cornmeal was scattered over the ground. In the middle of the spilt meal were giant dog prints. These dog prints were so large that the elderly couple knew this was no ordinary dog.

They immediately alerted the people of the village. It was decided that this must be a spirit dog from another world. The people did not want the spirit dog coming to their village. They decided to get rid of the dog by frightening it so bad it would never return. They gathered their drums and turtle shell rattles and later that night they hid around the area where the cornmeal was kept.

Late into the night they heard a whirring sound like many bird wings. They look up to see the form of a giant dog swooping down from the sky. It landed near the basket and then began to eat great mouthfuls of cornmeal.

Suddenly the people jumped up beating and shaking their noise makers. The noise was so loud it sounded like thunder. The giant dog turned and began to run down the path. The people chased after him making the loudest noises they could. It ran to the top of a hill and leaped into the sky, the cornmeal spilling out the sides of its mouth.

The giant dog ran across the black night sky until it disappeared from sight. But the cornmeal that had spilled from its mouth made a path way across the sky. Each gain of cornmeal became a star.

The Cherokees call that pattern of stars, gi li' ut sun stan un' yi (gil-LEE-oot-soon stan-UNH-yee), "the place where the dog ran."

And that is how the Milky Way came to be.

The Snake with the Big Feet

Native American Lore

Long ago, in that far-off happy time when the world was new, and there were no white people at all, only Indians and animals, there was a snake who was different from other snakes. He had feet-big feet. And the other snakes, because he was different, hated him, and made life wretched for him. Finally, they drove him away from the country where the snakes lived, saying, "A good long way from here live other ugly creatures with feet like yours. Go and live with them!" And the poor, unhappy Snake had to go away.

For days and days, he travelled. The weather grew cold and food became hard to find. At last, exhausted, his feet cut and frostbitten, he lay down on the bank of a river to die.

The Deer, E-se-ko-to-ye, looked out of a willow thicket, and saw the Snake lying on the river bank. Pitying him, the deer took the Snake into his own lodge and gave him food and medicine for his bleeding feet.

The Deer told the Snake that there were indeed creatures with feet like his who would befriend him, but that some among these would be enemies whom it would be necessary to kill before he could reach safety.

He showed the Snake how to make a shelter for protection from the cold and taught him how to make moccasins of deerskin to protect his feet. And at dawn the Snake continued his journey.

The sun was far down the western sky, and it was bitter cold when the Snake made camp the next night. As he gathered boughs for a shelter, Kais-kap the porcupine appeared. Shivering, the Porcupine asked him, "Will you give me shelter in your lodge for the night?"

The Snake said, "It's very little that I have, but you are welcome to share it."

"I am grateful," said Kais-kap, "and perhaps I can do something for you. Those are beautiful moccasins, brother, but they do not match your skin. Take some of my quills, and make a pattern on them, for good luck." So they worked a pattern on the moccasins with the porcupine quills, and the Snake went on his way again.

As the Deer had told him, he met enemies. Three times he was challenged by hostile Indians, and three times he killed his adversary.

At last he met an Indian who greeted him in a friendly manner. The Snake had no gifts for this kindly chief, so he gave him the moccasins. And that, so the old Ones say, was how our people first learned to make moccasins of deerskin, and to ornament them with porcupine quills in patterns, like those on the back of a snake. And from that day on the Snake lived in the lodge of the chief, counting his coup of scalps with the warriors by the Council fire and, for a long time, was happy.

But the chief had a daughter who was beautiful and kind, and the Snake came to love her very much indeed. He wished that he were human, so that he might marry the maiden, and have his own lodge. He knew there was no hope of this unless the High Gods, the Above Spirits took pity on him, and would perform a miracle on his behalf.

So he fasted and prayed for many, many days. But all his fasting and praying had no result, and at last the Snake came very ill.

Now, in the tribe, there was a very highly skilled Medicine Man. Mo'ki-ya was an old man, so old that he had seen and known, and understood, everything that came within the compass of his people's lives, and many things that concerned the Spirits. Many times, his lodge was seen to sway with the Ghost Wind and the voices of those long gone on to the Sand Hills spoke to him.
Mo'ki-ya came to where the Snake lay in the chief's lodge, and sending all the others away, asked the Snake what his trouble was.

"It is beyond even your magic," said the Snake, but he told Mo'ki-ya about his love for the maiden, and his desire to become a man so that he could marry her.

Mo'ki-ya sat quietly thinking for a while. Then he said, "I shall go on a journey, brother. Perhaps my magic can help, perhaps not. We shall see when I return." And he gathered his medicine bundles and disappeared.

It was a long and fearsome journey that Mo'ki-ya made. He went to the shores of a great lake. He climbed a high mountain, and he took the matter to Nato'se, the Sun himself.

And Nato'se listened, for this man stood high in the regard of the spirits, and his medicine was good. He did not ask, and never had asked, for anything for himself, and to transform the Snake into a brave of the tribe was not a difficult task for the High Gods. The third day after the arrival of Mo'ki-ya at the Sun's abode, Nato'se said to him, "Return to your own lodge Mo'ki-ya, and build a fire of small sticks. Put many handfuls of sweet-grass on the fire, and when the smoke rises thickly, lay the body of the Snake in the middle of it."

And Mo'ki-ya came back to his own land.

The fire was built in the center of the Medicine lodge, as the Sun had directed, and when the sweetgrass smoldered among the embers, sending the smoke rolling in great billows through the tepee, Mo'ki-ya gently lifted the Snake, now very nearly dead, and placed him in the fire so that he was hidden by the smoke.

The Medicine-drum whispered softly in the dusk of the lodge: the chant of the old men grew a little louder, and then the smoke obscuring the fire parted like a curtain, and a young man stepped out.

Great were the rejoicings in the camp that night. The Snake, now a handsome young brave, was welcomed into the tribe with the ceremonies befitting the reception of one shown to be high in the favor of the spirits. The chief gladly gave him his daughter, happy to have a son law of such distinction.

Many brave sons and beautiful daughters blessed the lodge of the Snake and at last, so the Old ones say, his family became a new tribe-the Pe-sik-na-ta-pe, or Snake Indians.

The Origin of the Pleiades and the Pine
Cherokee Version

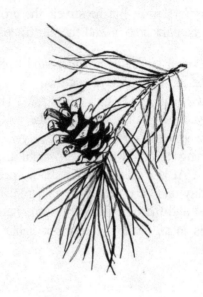

Long ago, when the world was new, there were seven boys who used to spend all their time down by the townhouse playing the gatayû'stï game, rolling a stone wheel along the ground and sliding a curved stick after it to strike it. Their mothers scolded, but it did no good, so one day they collected some gatayû'stï stones and boiled them in the pot with the corn for dinner. When the boys came home hungry their mothers dipped out the stones and said, "Since you like the gatayû'stï better than the cornfield, take the stones now for your dinner."

The boys were very angry, and went down to the townhouse, saying, "As our mothers treat us this way, let us go where we shall never trouble them any more." They began to dance, some say it was the Feather Dance and went round and round the townhouse, praying to the spirits to help them. At last their mothers were afraid something was wrong and went out to look for them. They saw the boys still dancing around the townhouse, and as they watched they noticed that their feet were off the earth, and that with every round they rose higher and higher in the air. They ran to get their children, but it was too late, for they were already above the roof of the townhouse, all but one, whose mother managed to pull him down with the gatayû'stï pole, but he struck the ground with such a force that he sank into it and the earth closed over him.

The other six circled higher and higher until they went up to the sky, Where we see them now as the Pleiades, which the Cherokee still call Ani'tsutsâ (The Boys). The people grieved long after them, but the mother whose boy had gone into the ground came every morning and every evening to cry over the spot until the earth was damp with tears. At last a little green shoot sprouted up and grew day by day until it became the tall tree that we call now the pine, and the pine is of the same nature as the stars and holds in itself the same bright light.

Falling-Star
A Cheyenne Legend

One day in the long ago, two young Indian girls were lying on the grass outside their tepee on a warm summer evening. They were looking up into the sky, describing star-pictures formed by their imaginations.

"That is a pretty star. I like that one," said First Girl.

"I like that one best of all--over there," Second Girl pointed.

First Girl pointed to the brightest star in the sky and said, "I like the brightest one best of all. That is the one I want to marry."

That evening they agreed to go out the next day to gather wood. Next morning they started for the timbered area. On their way they saw a porcupine climb a tree.

"I'll climb the tree and pull him down," said First Girl. She climbed but could not reach the porcupine.

Every time she stretched her hand for him, the porcupine climbed a little higher. Then the tree started growing taller. Second Girl below called to her friend, "Please come down, the tree is growing taller!"

"No," said First Girl as the porcupine climbed higher and the tree grew taller. Second Girl could see what was happening, so she ran back to the camp and told her people. They rushed to the tree, but First Girl had completely disappeared!

The tree continued to grow higher and higher. Finally, First Girl reached another land. She stepped off the tree branch and walked upon the sky! Before long she met a kindly looking middle-aged man who spoke to her. First Girl began to cry.

"Whatever is the matter? Only last night I heard you wish that you could marry me. I am the Brightest-Star," he said.

First Girl was pleased to meet Brightest-Star and became happy again when she got her wish and married him. He told her that she could dig roots with the other star-women, but to beware of a certain kind of white turnip with a great green top. This kind she must never dig. To do so was "against the medicine"--against the rules of the Sky-Chief.

Every day First Girl dug roots. Her curiosity about the strange white turnip became so intense that she decided to dig up one of them. It took her a long, long time. When she finally pulled out the root, a huge hole was left. She looked into the hole and far, far below she saw the camp of her own people.

Everything and everyone was very small, but she could see lodges and people walking. Instantly she became homesick to see her own people again. How could she ever get down from the sky? She realized it was a long, long way down to earth. Then her eyes fell upon the long tough grass growing near her. Could she braid it into a long rope? She decided to try, every day pulling more long grass and braiding more rope.

One time her husband Brightest-Star asked, "What is it that keeps you outdoors so much of the time?"

"I walk a great distance and that makes me tired. I need to sit down and rest before I can start back home."

At last she finished making her strong rope, thinking by now it must be long enough. She tied one end of the rope to a log that she rolled across the top of the hole as an anchor. She let down the rope. It looked as though it touched the ground.

She lowered herself into the hole, holding onto the braided rope. It seemed to take a long time as she slowly lowered herself until she came to the end of the rope. But it did not touch the earth! For a long while she hung on dangling in midair and calling uselessly for help. When she could hold on no longer, she fell to the ground and broke into many pieces. Although she died, her unborn son did not die, because he was made of star-stone and did not break.

A meadowlark saw what happened and took the falling-star baby to her nest. There the lark kept him with her own baby birds. When they were older, Falling-Star crept out of the nest with the little birds. The stronger the birds grew, the stronger grew Falling-Star. Soon all of them could crawl and run. The young birds practiced their flying while Falling-Star ran after them. Then the young birds could fly anywhere they wished, while Falling-Star ran faster and faster to keep up with them.

"Son, you had better go home to your own people," said Mother Meadowlark. "It is time for us to fly south for the winter. Before long, the weather here will be very cold."

"Mother Meadowlark," asked Falling-Star. "Why do you want me to leave you? I want to go with you."

"No, Son," she replied. "You must go home now."

"I will go if Father Meadowlark will make me a bow and some arrows."

Father Meadowlark made a bow and pulled some of his own quills to feather the arrows. He made four arrows and a bow for Falling- Star. Then he started Falling-Star in the right direction toward his home, downstream.

Falling-Star travelled a long time before he reached the camp of his people. He went into the nearest lodge owned by an old grandmother.

"Grandmother," he said. "I need a drink of water."

"My grandson," she said to him, "only the young men who are the fastest runners can go for water. There is a water-monster who sucks up any people who go too close to it."

"Grandmother, if you will give me your buffalo-pouch and your buffalo-horn ladle, I will bring you water."

"Grandson, I warn you that many of our finest young men have been destroyed by the water-monster. I fear that you will be killed, too." But she gave him the things he asked for. He went upstream and dipped water, at the same time keeping watch for the monster.

At the very moment Falling-Star filled his bucket, the Water-monster raised its head above the water. His mouth was enormous. He sucked in his breath and drew in Falling-Star, the bucket, water, and the ladle. When Falling-Star found himself inside the monster's stomach, he saw all the other people who had ever been swallowed. With his Star-stone, he cut a hole in the animal's side. Out crawled all the people and Falling-Star rescued his pouch and ladle for his grandmother, taking her some cool, fresh water.

"My grandson, who are you?" she asked, marveling at his survival.

"Grandmother, I am Falling-Star. I killed the monster that has caused our people much suffering, and I rescued all the people who had been swallowed."

The old woman told the village crier to spread the good news that the monster was dead. Now that Falling-Star had saved the camp people there, he asked the grandmother, "Are there other camps of our people nearby?"

"Yes, there is one farther downstream," she said.

Falling-Star took his bow and arrows and left camp. The fall of the year had now arrived. After travelling many days, he reached the other camp. Again he went into an old woman's lodge where she sat near her fire.

"Grandmother, I am very hungry," he said.

"My son, my son, we have no food. We cannot get any buffalo meat. Whenever our hunters go out for buffalo, a great white crow warns the buffalo, which drives them away.

"How sad," he said. "I will try to help. Go out and look for
a worn-out buffalo robe with little hair. Tell your chief to
choose two of his fastest runners and send them to me."

Later, the old woman returned with the robe and the two
swift runners. Falling-Star told them his plan. "I will go to a
certain place and wait for the buffalo. When the herd runs, I
will follow, disguised as a buffalo in the worn-out robe.
You two runners chase me and the buffalo for a long
distance. When you overtake me, you must shoot at me. I
will pretend to be dead. You pretend to cut me open and
leave me there on the ground."

When the real buffalo arrived, the white crow flew over
them screaming, "They are coming! They are after you!
Run, run!" The buffalo herd ran, followed by a shabby-
looking bull.

The two swift runners chased the old bull according to
plan. All kinds of birds, wolves, and coyotes came toward
the carcass from all directions. Among them was the white
crow. As he flew over Falling-Star in disguise, he called
out shrilly, "I wonder if this is Falling-Star?"

Time after time the crow flew over the carcass, still calling,
"I wonder if this is Falling-Star?" He came closer and
closer with each pass. When he was close enough, Falling-
Star sprang and grabbed the legs of the white crow. All of
the other birds and animals scattered in every direction.

When Falling-Star brought the captive white crow home to
the grandmother, she sent word for the chief.

"I will take the white crow to my lodge. I will tie him to the
smoke hole and smoke him dead," said the chief.

From that moment on, the good Cheyenne were able to kill many buffalo and they had plenty of buffalo meat for all their needs.

The people in gratitude gave Falling-Star a lovely lodge-home and a pretty Indian maiden waiting there to become his wife. They remained all of their lives with the Northern Cheyenne Indian tribe.

The Story of the Land of Northern Lights

Algonquin
"The Native American Story of the Land of Northern Lights" from "The Red Indian Fairy Book" by Frances Jenkins Olcott 1917

Once there was a Wabanaki Chief who had an only son. The boy worried his parents very much because he never played with other boys and girls in the village. Every few days he took down his bow and arrows from the side of the wigwam, and went away, no one knew where. And when he came back, his mother and father asked him: "Where have you been? What have you seen?" And he never answered a word.

One day the Chief said to his wife: "Our son must be watched. I will follow him."

So the next time the boy took down the bow and arrows, his father followed in his path. They travelled along for some time, until the Chief felt himself walking over a trail of dim, white light. Then his eyes were closed by invisible power, and he saw nothing more.

When he could open his eyes again, he was standing in a strange country lighted by dim, white light, and the people walking about him were different from any he had ever seen before. And near him were many white wigwams.

While the Chief was looking around, an old man stepped up to him, and said, "Do you know what land this is?"

"No," said the Chief.

"You are in the Land of the Northern Lights," replied the old man. "I came here many years ago from the lower country. I walked along the Milky Way, which is the same trail over which you came. There is a boy who comes every few days over that path, to play with our people."

"That boy is my son," said the Chief, "where may I find him? And how may we return in safety to the lower country?"

"You will soon see your son playing with our people, and if you wish it, the Chief of the Northern Lights will send you both home safely."

Then the Chief saw that a ball-game was beginning. Many braves came from the wigwams. They wore around their waists belts made of rainbows, and from their heads arose lights of every color.

And as they threw the ball, the lights from their belts and heads shot up against the dim, white sky. Flashes of rose, violet, green, yellow, orange, and red, quivered, leaped, and danced against the Sky, and died down. And then the flashes shot upward again, flickering and dancing. And the brave, with the brightest lights upon his head, was the Chief's son.

While the Chief was watching the game, the old man went to the wigwam of the Chief of the Northern Lights, and said, "There is a man here from the lower country, who wishes to return to his home, and take his son with him."

So the Chief of the Northern Lights called all his people together, and bade them give back the boy to his father. Then he summoned two great birds and told them to carry the boy and man back in safety to the lower country.

One bird lifted up the boy, and the other took up his father, and they flew away with them along the Milky Way. The Chief felt his eyes closed again, and when he could open them, he was standing with his son, near his own wigwam.

And after that the boy taught the men of the village the ball-game. And that is how the Wabanaki say they learned to play ball.

The Hunting of the Great Bear

There were four hunters who were brothers. No hunters
were as good as they at following a trail. They never gave
up once they began tracking their quarry.

One day, in the moon when the cold nights return, an
urgent message came to the village of the four hunters. A
great bear, one so large and powerful that many thought it
must be some kind of monster, had appeared. The people of
the village whose hunting grounds the monster had invaded
were afraid. The children no longer went out to play in the
woods. The long houses of the village were guarded each
night by men with weapons who stood by the entrances.
Each morning, when the people went outside, they found
the huge tracks of the bear in the midst of their village.
They knew that soon it would become even more bold.

Picking up their spears and calling to their small dog, the
four hunters set forth for that village, which was not far
away. As they came closer they noticed how quiet the
woods were. There were no signs of rabbits or deer and
even the birds were silent. On a great pine tree they found
the scars where the great bear had reared up on hind legs
and made deep scratches to mark its territory. The tallest of
the brothers tried to touch the highest of the scratch marks
with the tip of his spear. "It is as the people feared," the
first brother said. "This one we are to hunt is Nyah-gwaheh,
a monster bear."

"But what about the magic that the Nyah-gwaheh has?"
said the second brother.

The first brother shook his head. "That magic will do it no
good if we find its track."

"That's so," said the third brother. "I have always heard that from the old people. Those creatures can only chase a hunter who has not yet found its trail. When you find the track of the Nyah-gwaheh and begin to chase it, then it must run from you."

"Brothers," said the fourth hunter who was the fattest and laziest, "did we bring along enough food to eat? It may take a long time to catch this big bear. I'm feeling hungry."

Before long, the four hunters and their small dog reached the village. It was a sad sight to see. There was no fire burning in the center of the village and the doors of all the long houses were closed. Grim men stood on guard with clubs and spears and there was no game hung from the racks or skins stretched for tanning. The people looked hungry.

The elder sachem of the village came out and the tallest of the four hunters spoke to him.

"Uncle," the hunter said, "we have come to help you get rid of the monster."

Then the fattest and laziest of the four brothers spoke. "Uncle," he said, "is there some food we can eat? Can we find a place to rest before we start chasing this big bear? I'm tired."

The first hunter shook his head and smiled. "My brother is only joking, Uncle." he said. "We are going now to pick up the monster bear's trail."

"I am not sure you can do that, Nephews," the elder sachem said. "Though we find tracks closer and closer to the doors

of our lodges each morning, whenever we try to follow
those tracks they disappear."

The second hunter knelt down and patted the head of their
small dog. "Uncle," he said, that is because they do not
have a dog such as ours." He pointed to the two black
circles above the eyes of the small dog. "Four-Eyes can see
any tracks, even those many days old."

"May Creator's protection be with you," said the elder
sachem.

"Do not worry. Uncle," said the third hunter. "Once we are
on a trail we never stop following until we've finished our
hunt." "That's why I think we should have something to eat
first," said the fourth hunter, but his brothers did not listen.
They nodded to the elder sachem and began to leave.
Sighing, the fattest and laziest of the brothers lifted up his
long spear and trudged after them.

They walked, following their little dog. It kept lifting up its
head, as if to look around with its four eyes. The trail was
not easy to find.

"Brothers," the fattest and laziest hunter complained, "don't
you think we should rest. We've been walking a long time."
But his brothers paid no attention to him. Though they
could see no tracks, they could feel the presence of the
Nyah-gwaheh. They knew that if they did not soon find its
trail, it would make its way behind them. Then they would
be the hunted ones.

The fattest and laziest brother took out his pemmican
pouch. At least he could eat while they walked along. He
opened the pouch and shook out the food he had prepared
so carefully by pounding together strips of meat and berries

with maple sugar and then drying them in the sun. But instead of pemmican, pale squirming things fell out into his hands. The magic of the Nyah-gwaheh had changed the food into worms.

"Brothers," the fattest and laziest of the hunters shouted, "let's hurry up and catch that big bear! Look what it did to my pemmican. Now I'm getting angry."

Meanwhile, like a pale giant shadow, the Nyah-gwaheh was moving through the trees close to the hunters. Its mouth was open as it watched them and its huge teeth shone, its eyes flashed red. Soon it would be behind them and on their trail.

Just then, though, the little dog lifted its head and yelped. "Eh-heh!" the first brother called.

"Four-Eyes has found the trail," shouted the second brother.

"We have the track of the Nyah-gwaheh," said the third brother.

"Big Bear," the fattest and laziest one yelled, "we are after you, now!"

Fear filled the heart of the great bear for the first time and it began to run. As it broke from the cover of the pines, the four hunters saw it, a gigantic white shape, so pale as to appear almost naked. With loud hunting cries, they began to run after it. The great bear's strides were long and it ran more swiftly than a deer. The four hunters and their little dog were swift also though and they did not fall behind. The trail led through the swamps and the thickets. It was easy to read, for the bear pushed everything aside as it ran, even knocking down big trees. On and on they ran, over hills and through valleys. They came to the slope of a mountain and followed the trail higher and higher, every now and then catching a glimpse of their quarry over the next rise.

Now though the lazy hunter was getting tired of running. He pretended to fall and twist his ankle.

"Brothers," he called, "I have sprained my ankle. You must carry me."

So his three brothers did as he asked, two of them carrying him by turns while the third hunter carried his spear. They ran more slowly now because of their heavy load, but they were not falling any further behind. The day had turned now into night, yet they could still see the white shape of the great bear ahead of them. They were at the top of the mountain now and the ground beneath them was very dark as they ran across it. The bear was tiring, but so were they. It was not easy to carry their fat and lazy brother. The little dog, Four-Eyes, was close behind the great bear, nipping at its tail as it ran.

"Brothers," said the fattest and laziest one. "Put me down now. I think my leg has gotten better."

The brothers did as he asked. Fresh and rested, the fattest and laziest one grabbed his spear and dashed ahead of the others. Just as the great bear turned to bite at the little dog, the fattest and laziest hunter leveled his spear and thrust it into the heart of the Nyah-Gwaheh. The monster bear fell dead.

By the time the other brothers caught up, the fattest and laziest hunter had already built a fire and was cutting up the big bear.

"Come on, brothers," he said. "Let's eat. All this running has made me hungry!"

So they cooked the meat of the great bear and its fat sizzled as it dripped from their fire. They ate until even the fattest and laziest one was satisfied and leaned back in contentment. Just then, though, the first hunter looked down at his feet.

"Brothers," he exclaimed, "look below us!"

The four hunters looked down. Below them were thousands of small sparkling lights in the darkness which they realized, were all around them.

"We aren't on a mountain top at all," said the third brother. "We are up in the sky." And it was so. The great bear had indeed been magical. Its feet had taken it high above the earth as it tried to escape the four hunters. However, their determination not to give up the chase had carried them up that strange trail.

Just then their little dog yipped twice.

"The great bear!" said the second hunter. "Look!"

The hunters looked. There, where they had piled the bones of their feast the Great Bear was coming back to life and rising to its feet. As they watched, it began to run again, the small dog close on its heels.

"Follow me," shouted the first brother. Grabbing up their spears, the four hunters again began to chase the great bear across the skies.

So it was, the old people say, and so it still is. Each autumn the hunters chase the great bear across the skies and kill it. Then, as they cut it up for their meal, the blood falls down from the heavens and colors the leaves of the maple trees scarlet. They cook the bear and the fat dripping from their fires turns the grass white.

If you look carefully into the skies as the seasons change, you can read that story. The great bear is the square shape some call the bowl of the Big Dipper. The hunters and their small dog (which you can just barely see) are close behind, the dipper's handle. When autumn comes and that constellation turns upside down, the old people say. "Ah, the lazy hunter has killed the bear." But as the moons pass and the sky moves once more towards spring, the bear slowly rises back on its feet and the chase begins again.

How the Great Chiefs Made the Moon and the Sun

Hopi

Once upon a time, when our people first came up from the villages of the underworld, there was no sun. There was no moon. They saw only dreary darkness and felt the coldness. They looked hard for firewood, but in the darkness they found little.

One day as they stumbled around, they saw a light in the distance. The Chief sent a messenger to see what caused the light. As the messenger approached it, he saw a small field containing corn, beans, squash, watermelons, and other foods. All around the field a great fire was burning. Nearby stood a straight, handsome man wearing around his neck a turquoise necklace of four strands. Turquoise pendants hung from his ears.

"Who are you?" the owner of the field asked the messenger.

"My people and I have come from the cave world below," the messenger replied. "And we suffer from the lack of light and the lack of food."

"My name is Skeleton," said the owner of the field. He showed the stranger the terrible mask he often wore and then gave him some food. "Now return to your people and guide them to my field."

When all the people had arrived, Skeleton began to give them food from his field. They marveled that, although the crops seemed so small, there was enough food for everyone. He gave them ears of corn for roasting; he gave them beans, squashes, and watermelons. The people built fires for themselves and were happy.

Later, Skeleton helped them prepare fields of their own and to make fires around them. There they planted corn and soon harvested a good crop.

"Now we should move on," the people said. "We want to find the place where we will live always."

Away from the fires it was still dark. The Great Chiefs, at a council with Skeleton, decided to make a moon like the one they had enjoyed in the underworld.

They took a piece of well-prepared buffalo hide and cut from it a great circle. They stretched the circle tightly over a wooden hoop and then painted it carefully with white paint. When it was entirely dry, they mixed some black paint and painted, all around its edge, completing the picture of the moon. When all of this was done, they attached a stick to the disk and placed it on a large square of white cloth. Thus they made a symbol of the moon.

Then the Great Chiefs selected one of the young men and bade him to stand on top of the moon symbol. They took up the cloth by its corners and began to swing it back and forth, higher and higher. As they were swinging it, they

sang a magic song. Finally, with a mighty heave, they
threw the moon disk upward. It continued to fly swiftly,
upward and eastward.

As the people watched, they suddenly saw light in the
eastern sky. The light became brighter and brighter. Surely
something was burning there, they thought. Then
something bright with light rose in the east. That was the
moon!

Although the moon made it possible for the people to move
around with less stumbling, its light was so dim that
frequently the workers in the fields would cut up their food
plants instead of the weeds. It was so cold that fires had to
be kept burning around the fields all the time.

Again the Great Chiefs held a council with Skeleton, and
again they decided that something better must be done.

This time, instead of taking a piece of buffalo hide, they
took a piece of warm cloth that they themselves had woven
while they were still in the underworld. They fashioned this
as they had fashioned the disk of buffalo hide, except that
this time they painted the face of the circle with a copper-
colored paint.

They painted eyes and a mouth on the disk and decorated
the forehead with colors that the Great Chiefs decided upon
according to their desires. Around the circle, they then
wove a ring of corn husks, arranged in a zig zag design.
Around the circle of corn husks, they threaded a string of
red hair from some animal. To the back of the disk, they
fastened a small ring of corn husks. Through that ring they
poked a circle of eagle feathers.

To the top of each eagle feather, the old Chief tied a few little red feathers taken from the top of the head of a small bird. On the forehead of the circle, he attached an abalone shell. Then the sun disk was completed.

Again the Great Chiefs chose a young man to stand on top of the disk, which they had placed on a large sheet. As they had done with the moon disk, they raised the cloth by holding its corners. Then they swung the sun disk back and forth, back and forth, again and again. With a mighty thrust, they threw the man and the disk far into the air. It travelled fast into the eastern sky and disappeared.

All the people watched it carefully. In a short time, they saw light in the east as if a great fire were burning. Soon the new sun rose and warmed the earth with its kindly rays.

Now with the moon to light the earth at night and the sun to light and warm it by day, all the people decided to pick up their provisions and go on. As they started, the White people took a trail that led them far to the south. The Hopis took one to the north, and the Pueblos took one midway between the two. Thus they wandered on to the places where they were to live.

The Hopis wandered a long time, building houses and planting crops until they reached the mesas where they now live. The ruins of the ancient villages are scattered to the very beginnings of the great river of the canyon--the Colorado.

Tale of Coyote Regulates Life After Death

The people had many councils from time to time. The errand man went all round to call the people to these councils.

At one council Coyote arose and said: "First, we must change our rule about death, because all are not being treated alike. Now when some die they come back to their people, and then others die and never see their people again. I propose to make another rule, so that we may all be treated alike after death. This is the rule that I wish to propose: When any one dies let him be dead forever, and let no living person ever see him again. Our Great-Father-Above made a place there where every one of us may go after death. Now when any one dies he shall go from the living forever, but we shall still keep up the fire for six days."

All the people were well pleased with Coyote's rule, and so from that time on, even to the present day, the same rule is kept, and when anybody dies he is gone forever, never to return again. The people are taken to the sky when they die and become the stars that we see at night.

Morning Star, who freed the earth from bad animals, had three brothers, and he was the oldest one and the leader of all the tribe. In the beginning he had been the errand man, and during war expeditions he had to get up early in the morning, hours before dawn, to go around the camps and wake the people, so that the enemy would not find them. That is the reason he gets up so early now.

In the evening one of his brothers would go back a long distance to see if the enemy was coming on their trail, and so the man was named Evening Star. The other two brothers were named North Star and South Star, and these four brothers always had something to do. North Star always had to camp in the North and watch for the enemy lest they should approach from that direction; South Star had to camp in the South and watch lest the enemy should approach from that direction. Their father's name was Great Star, and he was the chief of the people. Now the people think that when any one dies he goes up to the sky, where he turns around and looks back and becomes one of the stars, and so they believe every one when he dies goes up to the sky.

They That Chase After the Bear

This version of the legend comes from William Jones' 1907 collection of Mesquakie stories, Fox Texts.

It is said that once on a time long ago in the winter, at the beginning of the season of snow after the first fall of snow, three men went on a hunt for game early on a morning. Upon a hillside into a place where the bush was thick a bear they trailed. One of the men went in following the trail of the bear. And then he started it up running. "Towards the place whence comes the cold is he speeding away!" he said to his companions.

He that headed off on the side which lay towards the source of the cold, "In the direction of the place of the noonday sky is he running!" he said.

Back and forth amongst themselves they kept the bear fleeing. They say that after a while he that was coming up behind chanced to look down at the ground. Behold, green was the surface of the earth lying face up! Now of a truth up into the sky were they conveyed by the bear! When round about the bush they were chasing it then truly was the time that up into the sky they went. And then he that came up behind cried out to him that was next ahead: "O River-that-joins-Another, let us go back! We are being carried up into the sky!" Thus said he to River-that-joins-Another. But by him was he not heeded.

Now River-that-joins-Another was he who ran in between the two and a little puppy Hold-Tight he had for a pet.

In the autumn they overtook the bear, and then they slew it. After they had slain it, then boughs of the oak they cut, likewise boughs of the sumac, then laying the bear on top of the leaves they flayed and cut up the bear; after they had flayed and cut it up, then they began slinging and scattering the meat in every direction. Towards the place of the coming of the morning they flung the head; in the winter-time when the morning is about to appear some stars usually rise; it is said that they came from the head of the bear. And also his backbone, towards the place of the morning they flung it too. They too are commonly seen in the winter-time; they are stars that lie huddled close together; it is said that they came from the backbone.

And they say that these four stars in the lead were the bear, and the three stars at the rear were they who were chasing after the bear. In between two of them is a tiny little star, it hangs near by another; they say that it was the puppy, the pet Hold-Tight of River-that-joins-Another.

Every autumn the oaks and sumacs redden in the leaf because it is then that the hunters lay the bear on top of the leaves and flay and cut it up; then red with blood become the leaves. Such is the reason why every autumn red become the leaves of the oaks and sumacs.

That is the end of the story.

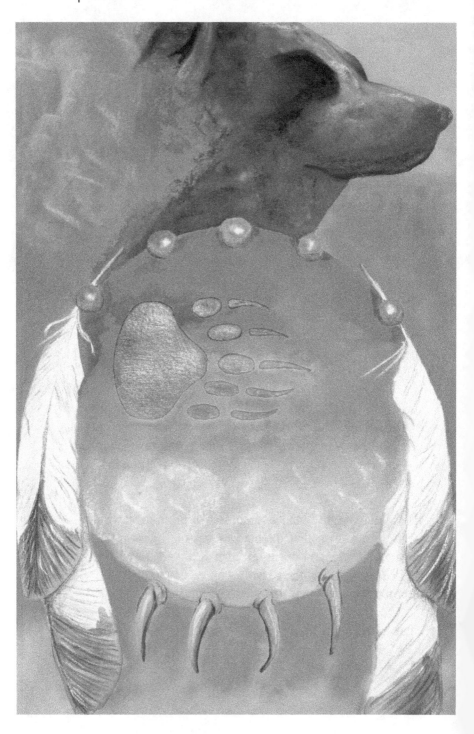

Tale of the Lazy Boys Who Became the Pleiades

*Dorsey, George A. Traditions of the Caddo. Washington:
Carnegie Institution. 1905.*

Long, long ago, in the beginning of this world, there lived
an old woman with seven children, who were all boys. The
boys were full of life and fun and they would go away from
the others and play all the day long, and would not work,
nor take time to eat but twice a day-morning and evening.

When they came home in the evening their mother would
scold them, and one evening when they came home late for
their supper their mother would not let them have anything
to eat. The boys were very angry and went back to their
play and determined on the morrow to go away where they
would never trouble her any more.

The next morning early they went down to their playground
before breakfast and began to go round and round the
house, praying to the spirits to help them. At last their

mother noticed and heard what they were saying, and as she watched them she noticed that their feet were off the earth, and then she knew that something was wrong, and she ran out trying to get her children, but it was too late.

With every round they rose higher and higher in the air, and were soon above the roof of the house. They circled higher and higher until they went up to the sky, where we can see them now as the Seven Stars. These seven boys who were taken to the sky were very indolent, and when the work time came they would always slip off and play. That is the reason that during the winter months the Seven Stars can be seen; but at the beginning of the spring months, at the work time, the Seven Stars are gone.

The Sun Tests His Son-in-law

A Bella Coola Legend
Boas, Jesup North Pacific
Expedition, i, 73

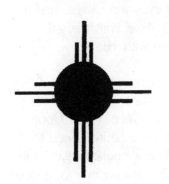

In a place on Bella Coola River, there used to be a salmon-weir. A chief and his wife lived at this place. One day the wife was cutting salmon on the bank of the river. When she opened the last salmon, she found a small boy in it.

She took him out and washed him in the river. She placed him near by, entered the house, and said to the people, "Come and see what I have found in my salmon!" She had a child in her house, which was still in the cradle.

The little boy whom she had found was half as long as her fore-arm. She carried him into the house, and the people advised her to take good care of him. She nursed him with her own baby.

When the people were talking in the house, the baby looked around as though he understood what they were saying. On the following day the people were surprised to see how much he had grown, and in a few days he was as tall as any ordinary child. Her own baby also grew up with marvelous rapidity. She gave each of them one breast. After a few days they were able to walk and to talk.

The two young men were passing by the houses, and looked into the doorways. There was a house in the center of this town; there they saw a beautiful girl sitting in the middle of the house. Her hair was red, and reached down to the floor. She was very white. Her eyes were large, and as clear as rock crystal. The boy fell in love with the girl. They went on, but his thoughts were with her.

The Salmon boy said, "I am going to enter this house. You must watch closely what I do, and imitate me. The Door of this house tries to bite every one who enters." The Door opened, and the Salmon jumped into the house. Then the Door snapped, but missed him. When it opened again, the boy jumped into the house. They found a number of people inside, who invited them to sit down. They spread food before them, but the boy did not like their food. It had a very strong smell, and looked rather curious. It consisted of algae that grow on logs that lie in the river.

When the boy did not touch it, one of the men said to him, "Maybe you want to eat those two children. Take them down to the river and throw them into the water, but do not look."

The two children arose, and he took them down to the river. Then he threw them into the water without looking at them. At the place where he had thrown them down, he found a male and a female Salmon. He took them up to the house and roasted them.

The people told him to preserve the intestines and the bones carefully. After he had eaten, one of the men told him to carry the intestines and the bones to the same place where he had thrown the children into the water. He carried them in his hands, and threw them into the river without looking. When he entered the house, he heard the children following him. The girl was covering one of her eyes with her hands.

The boy was limping, because he had lost one of his bones.

Then the people looked at the place where the boy had been sitting, and they found the eye, and a bone from the head of the male salmon. They ordered the boy to throw these into the water. He took the children and the eye and the bone, and threw them into the river. Then the children were hale and well.

After a while the youth said to his Salmon brother, "I wish to go to the other house where I saw the beautiful girl." They went there, and he said to his Salmon brother, "Let us enter. I should like to see her face well."

They went in. Then the man arose, and spread a caribou blanket for them to sit on, and the people gave them food. Then he whispered to his brother, "Tell the girl I want to marry her." The Salmon boy told the girl, who smiled, and said, "He must not marry me. Whoever marries me must die. I like him, and I do not wish to kill him; but if he wishes to die, let him marry me.

The woman was the Salmon-berry Bird. After one day she gave birth to a boy, and on the following day she gave birth to a girl. She was the daughter of the Spring Salmon.

After a while the girl's father said, "Let us launch our canoe, and let us carry the young man back to his own people." He sent a messenger to call all the people of the village; and they all made themselves ready, and early the next morning they started in their canoes. The young man went in the canoe of the Spring Salmon, which was the fastest.

The canoe of the Sock-eye Salmon came next. The people in the canoe of the Calico Salmon were laughing all the time. They went up the river; and a short distance below the village of the young man's father they landed, and made fast their canoes. Then they sent two messengers up the river to see if the people had finished their salmon-weir.

Soon they returned with information that the weir had been finished. Then they sent the young man and his wife, and they gave them a great many presents for the young man's father.

The watchman who was stationed at the salmon-weir saw two beautiful salmon entering the trap. They were actually the canoes of the salmon; but they looked to him like two salmon. Then the watchman put the traps down over the weir, and he saw a great many fish entering them. He raised the trap when it was full, and took the fish out.

The young man thought, "I wish he would treat me and my wife carefully", and his wish came true. The man broke the heads of the other salmon, but he saved the young man and his wife. Then he carried the fish up to the house, and hung them over a pole.

During the night the young man and his wife resumed their human shape. The youth entered his father's house. His head was covered with eagle-down. He said to his father, "I am the fish whom you caught yesterday. Do you remember the time when you lost me? I have lived in the country of the Salmon. The Salmon accompanied me here. They are staying a little farther down the river. It pleases the Salmon to see the people eating fish." And, turning to his mother, he continued, "You must be careful when cutting Salmon.

Never break any of their bones, but preserve them, and throw them into the water." The two children of the young man had also entered into the salmon-trap. He put some leaves on the ground, placed red and white cedar-bark over them, and covered them with eagle-down, and he told his mother to place the Salmon upon these.

As soon as he had given these instructions, the Salmon
began to come up the river. They crossed the weir and
entered the traps. They went up the river as far as Stuick,
and the people dried the Salmon according to his
instructions. They threw the bones into the water, and the
Salmon returned to life, and went back to their own
country, leaving their meat behind.

The Cohoes Salmon had the slowest canoe, and therefore
he was the last to reach the villages. He gave many presents
to the Indians. He gave them many-colored leaves, and thus
caused the leaves of the trees to change color in the
autumn.

Now all the Salmon had returned. The Salmon-berry Bird
and her children had returned with them. Then the young
man made up his mind to build a small hut, from which he
intended to catch eagles. He used a long pole, to which a
noose was attached. The eagles were baited by means of
Salmon. He spread a mat in his little house, and when he
had caught an eagle he pulled out its down.

He accumulated a vast amount of down. Then he went back
to his house and asked his younger brother to accompany
him. When they came to the hut which he had used for
catching eagles, he gave the boy a small staff. Then he said
to him, "Do not be sorry when I leave you. I am going to
visit the Sun. I am not going to stay away a long time. I
staid long in the country of the Salmon, but I shall not stay
long in heaven.

I am going to lie down on this mat. Cover me with this
down, and then begin to beat time with your staff. You will
see a large feather flying upward, then stop." The boy

obeyed, and everything happened as he had said.

The boy saw the feather flying in wide circles. When it reached a great height, it began to soar in large circles, and finally disappeared in the sky. Then the boy cried, and went back to his mother. The young man who had ascended to heaven found there a large house. It was the House of Myths. There he resumed his human shape, and peeped in at the door. Inside he saw a number of people who were turning their faces toward the wall. They were sitting on a low platform in the rear of the house. In the right-hand corner of the house he saw a large fire, and women sitting around it.

He leaned forward and looked into the house. An old woman discovered him, and beckoned him to come to her. He stepped up to her, and she warned him by signs not to go to the rear of the house. She said, "Be careful!

The men in the rear of the house intend to harm you." She opened a small box, and gave him the bladder of a mountain-goat, which contained the cold wind. She told him to open the bladder if they should attempt to harm him. She said that if he opened it, no fire could burn him. She told him that the men were going to place him near the fire, in order to burn him; that one of them would wipe his face, then fire would come forth from the floor, scorching everything.

The old woman told him everything that the people were going to do. Now the man in the rear of the house turned round. He was the Sun himself. He was going to try the strength of the visitor. When he saw the young man, he said to the old woman, "Did anybody come to visit you? Let the young man come up to me. I wish him to sit down near me." The young man stepped up to the Sun, and as soon as he had sat down, the Sun wiped his face and looked at the young man (he had turned his face while he was wiping it).

Then the young man felt very hot. He tied his blanket tightly round his body, and opened the bladder which the woman had given him. Then the cold wind that blows down the mountains in the winter was liberated, and he felt cool and comfortable. The Sun had not been able to do him any harm. The old man did not say anything, but looked at his visitor.

After a while he said, "I wish to show you a little underground house that stands behind this house." They both rose and went outside. The small house had no door. Access was had to it by an opening in the center of the roof, through which a ladder led down to the floor. Not a breath of air entered this house. It was made of stone. When they had entered, the Sun made a small fire in the middle of the house; then he climbed up the ladder and closed the door, leaving his visitor inside. The Sun pulled up the ladder, in order to make escape impossible. Then the house began to grow very hot.

When the boy felt that he could not stand the heat any longer, he opened the bladder, and the cold wind came out; snow began to fall on the fire, which was extinguished; icicles began to form on the roof, and it was cool and comfortable inside. After a while the Sun said to his four daughters, "Go to the little underground house that stands behind our house, and sweep it," meaning that they were to remove the remains of the young man whom he believed to be burned.

They obeyed at once, each being eager to be the first to enter. When they opened the house, they were much surprised to find icicles hanging down from the roof.

When they were climbing down the ladder, the youth arose and scratched them. The youngest girl was the last to step down. The girls cried when the youth touched them, and ran away. The Sun heard their screams, and asked the reason.

He was much surprised and annoyed to hear that the young man was still alive. Then he devised another way of killing his visitor. He told his daughters to call him into his house. They went, and the young man re-entered the House of Myths. In the evening he lay down to sleep.

Then the Sun said to his daughters, "Early tomorrow morning climb the mountain behind our house. I shall tell the boy to follow you." The girls started while the visitor was still asleep. The girls climbed up to a small meadow which was near a precipice. They had taken the form of mountain-goats. When the Sun saw his daughters on the meadow, he called to his visitor, saying, "See those mountain-goats!" The young man arose when he saw the mountain-goats.

He wished to kill them. The Sun advised him to walk up the right-hand side of the mountain, saying that the left-hand side was dangerous. The young man carried his bow and arrow.

The Sun said, "Do not use your own arrows! Mine are much better." Then they exchanged arrows, the Sun giving him four arrows of his own. The points of these arrows were made of coal.

Now the young man began to climb the mountain. When he came up to the goats, he took one of the arrows, aimed it, and shot. It struck the animals, but fell down without killing it. The same happened with the other arrows. When he had spent all his arrows, they rushed up to him from the four sides, intending to kill him. His only way of escape was in the direction of the precipice. They rushed up to him, and pushed him down the steep mountain.

He fell headlong, but when he was halfway down he transformed himself into a ball of bird's down. He alighted gently on a place covered with many stones. There he resumed the shape of a man, arose, and ran into the house of the Sun to get his own arrows. He took them, climbed the mountain again, and found the mountain-goats on the same meadow. He shot them and killed them, and threw them down the precipice; then he returned. He found the goats at the foot of the precipice, and cut off their feet. He took them home.

He found the Sun sitting in front of the house. He offered him the feet, saying, "Count them, and see how many I have killed." The Sun counted them and now he knew that all his children were dead. Then he cried, "You killed my children!"

Then the youth took the bodies of the goats, fitted the feet on, and threw the bodies into a little river that was running past the place where they had fallen down. Thus they were restored to life.

He had learned this art in the country of the Salmon. Then he said to the girls, "Now run to see your father! He is wailing for you." They gave him a new name, saying, "He has restored us to life." The boy followed them. Then the Sun said, when he entered, "You shall marry my two eldest daughters."

On the next morning the people arose. Then the Sun said to them, "What shall I do to my son-in-law?" He called him,

and said, "Let us raise the trap of my salmon-weir." They
went up to the river in the Sun's canoe. The water of the
river was boiling. The youth was in the bow of the canoe,
while the Sun was steering. He caused the canoe to rock,
intending to throw the young man into the water. The water
formed a small cascade, running down over the weir. He
told the young man to walk over the top of the weir in order
to reach the trap.

He did so, walking over the top beam of the weir. When he
reached the baskets, the beam fell over, and he himself fell
into the water. The Sun saw him rise twice in the whirlpool
just below the weir. When he did not see him rise again, he
turned his canoe, and thought, "Now the boy has certainly
gone to Nuskyakek." The Sun returned to his house, and
said to his daughters, "I lost my son-in-law in the river. I
was not able to find him." Then his daughters were very
sad.

When the boy disappeared in the water, he was carried to
Nuskyakek; and he resumed the shape of a salmon while in
the water, and as soon as he landed he resumed human
shape and returned to his wife. The Sun saw him coming,
and was much surprised. In the evening they went to sleep.
On the following morning the Sun thought, "How can I kill
my son-in-law?" After a while he said to him, "Arise! We
will go and split wood for fuel."

He took his tools. They launched their canoe, and went
down the river to the sea. When they reached there, it was
perfectly calm. There were many snags embedded in the
mud in the mouth of the river, some of which were only
half submerged. They selected one of these snags a long
distance from the shore, and began to split it. Then the Sun
intentionally dropped his hammer into the water, and
thought at the same time, "Do not fall straight down, but

fall sideways, so that he will have much difficulty in
finding you." Then he sat down in his canoe, and said, "Oh!
I lost my old hammer. I had it at the time when the Sun was
created." He looked down into the water, and did not say a
word.

After a while he said to the young man, "Do you know how
to dive? Can you get my hammer? The water is not very
deep here."

The young man did not reply. Then the Sun continued, "I
will not go back without my hammer." Then the boy said,
"I know how to dive. If you so wish, I will try to get it."

The Sun promised to give him supernatural power if he was
able to bring the hammer back. The youth jumped into the
water, and then the Sun ordered the sea to rise, and he
called the cold wind to make the water freeze. It grew so
cold that a sheet of ice a fathom thick was formed at once
on top of the sea.

"Now," he thought, "I certainly have killed you!" He left
his canoe frozen up in the ice, and went home. He said to
his daughters, "I have lost my son-in-law. He drifted away
when the cold winds began to blow down the mountains. I
have also lost my little hammer."

But when he mentioned his hammer, his daughters knew at
once what had happened. The young man found the
hammer, and after he had obtained it he was going to return
to the canoe, but he struck his head against the ice, and was
unable to get out. He tried everywhere to find a crack.
Finally, he found a very narrow one. He transformed
himself into a fish, and came out of the crack. He jumped
about on the ice in the form of a fish, and finally resumed
his own shape.

He went back to the Sun's house, carrying the hammer. The Sun was sitting in front of the fire, his knees drawn up, and his legs apart. His eyes were closed, and he was warming himself. The young man took his hammer and threw it right against his stomach, saying, "Now take better care of your treasures."

The young man scolded the Sun, saying, "Now stop trying to kill me. If you try again, I shall kill you. Do you think I am an ordinary man? You cannot conquer me." The Sun did not reply.

In the evening he said to his son-in-law, "I hear a bird singing, which I should like very much to have."

The young man asked, "What bird is it?"

The Sun replied, "I do not know it. Watch it early to-morrow morning." The young man resolved to catch the bird. Very early in the morning he arose, and then he heard the bird singing outside. He knew at once that it was the ptarmigan. He left the house, and thought, "I wish you would come down!" Then the bird came down, and when it was quite near by he shot it. He hit one of its wings, intending to catch it alive.

He waited for the Sun to arise. The bird understood what the young man said, who thus spoke: "The chief here wishes to see you. Do not be afraid, I am not going to kill you. The chief has often tried to kill me, but he has been unable to do so.

You do not need to be afraid." The young man continued, "When it is dark I shall tell the Sun to ask you to sit near him, and when he is asleep I want you to peck out his eyes." When the Sun arose, the youth went into the house

carrying the bird, saying, "I have caught the bird; now I
hope you will treat it kindly. It will awaken us when it is
time to arise. When you lie down, let it sit down near you,
then it will call you in the morning."

In the evening the Sun asked the bird to sit down next to his
face. When he was asleep, the bird pecked out his eyes
without his knowing it. Early in the morning he heard the
bird singing. He was going to open his eyes, but he was not
able to do so. Then he called his son, saying, "The bird has
blinded me."

The young man jumped up and went to his father-in-law,
and said, "Why did you wish for the bird? Do you think it
is good? It is a bad bird. It has pecked out your eyes." He
took the bird and carried it outside, and thanked it for
having done as it was bidden. Then the bird flew away.

When it was time for the Sun to start on his daily course, he
said, "I am afraid I might fall, because I cannot see my
way." For four days he stayed in his house. He did not eat;
he was very sad. Then his son-in-law made up his mind to
cure him. He did not do so before, because he wanted to
punish him for his badness.

He took some water, and said to his father-in-law, "I will
try to restore your eyesight." He threw the water upon his
eyes, and at once his eyes were healed and well.

He said, "Now you can see what power I have. The water
with which I have washed my face has the power to heal
diseases. While I was in the country of the Salmon, I
bathed in the water in which the old Salmon bathed, in
order to regain youth; therefore the water in which I wash
makes everything young and well."
From this time on, the Sun did not try to do any harm to the

young man.

Finally, he wished to return to his father's village. He left
the house, and jumped down through the hole in heaven.
His wife saw him being transformed into a ball of eagle-
down, which floated down gently. Then her father told her
to climb as quickly as she could down his eyelashes. She
did so, and reached the ground at the same time as her
husband. He met his younger brother, who did not
recognize him. He had been in heaven for one year.

Tale of the Man and the Dog Who Became Stars

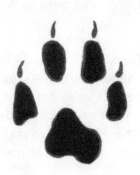

Dorsey, George A. Traditions of the Caddo. Washington: Carnegie Institution. 1905.

A young man had a Dog which he always took with him whenever he went to hunt. When he was at home he did not pay much attention to the Dog, and the Dog acted like any other dog, but when they were off alone the Dog would talk to his master just as if he were a man. He had the power of a prophet and could always tell what was going to happen.

One time, while they were out hunting, the Dog came running back to his master and told him that they were about to come to a very dangerous place. The young man asked where the place was, and the Dog said that he did not know just where it was, but that he knew it was not far away.

In another instant the Dog scented a deer and started out on its trail, and the man followed. Soon they came upon the deer. The man shot it, but only wounded it, and it continued to run until it reached the lake, and then jumped into the water. The Dog jumped in after it and soon caught it, because he could swim faster than the wounded deer. He held it while the young man threw off his clothes and swam to his assistance. Soon they killed the deer, and then the man put it on his shoulders and started to swim to the shore.

All at once the Dog cried out "Look out!" There before them and all around them were all kinds of poisonous and dangerous water animals. The man thought that they would surely be killed, for the animals were so numerous that they could not possibly swim past them. He began to pray to the spirits to help him, and as he prayed the water leaped up and threw them on the shore.

The young man felt so grateful to the spirits who had saved his and his Dog's lives that he cut some of the flesh from the deer and threw it into the water as a sacrifice. Then he and the Dog decided that they would not stay longer in this dangerous world, and so they went to the sky to live. There they can be seen as two bright stars in the south. The one to the east is the young man, and the one to the west is the Dog.

The Moon and the Thunders

A Cherokee Legend
Myths of the Cherokee,
James Mooney,
1900

The Sun was a young woman and lived in the East, while her brother, the Moon lived in the West. The girl had a lover who used to come every month in the dark of the moon to court her. He would come at night, and leave before daylight.

Although she talked with him she could not see his face in the dark, and he would not tell her his name, until she was wondering all the time who it could be.

At last she hit upon a plan to find out, so the next time he came, as they were sitting together in the dark of the âsi, she slyly dipped her hand into the cinders and ashes of the fireplace and rubbed it over his face, saying, "Your face is cold; you must have suffered from the wind," and pretending to be very sorry for him, but he did not know that she had ashes on her hand.

After a while he left her and went away again.

The next night when the Moon came up in the sky his face was covered with spots, and then his sister knew he was the one who had been coming to see her. He was so much ashamed to have her know it that he kept as far away as he could at the other end of the sky all the night. Ever since he tries to keep a long way behind the Sun, and when he does sometimes have to come near her in the west he makes himself as thin as a ribbon so that he can hardly be seen.

Some old people say that the moon is a ball which was thrown up against the sky in a game a long time ago.

They say that two towns were playing against each other, but one of them had the best runners and had almost won the game, when the leader of the other side picked up the ball with his hand--a thing that is not allowed in the game-- and tried to throw it to the goal, but it struck against the solid sky vault and was fastened there, to remind players never to cheat.

When the moon looks small and pale it is because some one has handled the ball unfairly, and for this reason they formerly played only at the time of a full moon.

When the sun or moon is eclipsed it is because a great frog up in the sky is trying to swallow it.

Everybody knows this, even the Creeks and the other tribes, and in the olden times, eighty or a hundred years ago, before the great medicine men were all dead, whenever they saw the sun grow dark the people would come together and fire guns and beat the drum, and in a little while this would frighten off the great frog and the sun would be all right again.

The common people call both Sun and Moon Nûñdä, one
being "Nûñdä that dwells in the day" and the other "Nûñdä
that dwells in the night," but the priests call the Sun
Su'tälidihï', "Six-killer," and the Moon Ge'`yägu'ga, though
nobody knows now what this word means, or why they use
these names. Sometimes people ask the Moon not to let it
rain or snow.

The great Thunder and his sons, the two Thunder boys, live
far in the west above the sky vault. The lightning and the
rainbow are their beautiful dress. The priests pray to the
Thunder and call him the Red Man, because that is the
brightest color of his dress.

There are other Thunders that live lower down, in the cliffs
and mountains, and under waterfalls, and travel on invisible
bridges from one high peak to another where they have
their town houses. The great Thunders above the sky are
kind and helpful when we pray to them, but these others are
always plotting mischief. One must not point at the
rainbow, or one's finger will swell at the lower joint.

Tale of Evening-Star and Orphan-Star

Dorsey, George A.
Traditions of the Caddo.
Washington: Carnegie
Institution. 1905.

A poor orphan boy lived with a large family of people who were not kind to him and mistreated him. He could not go to play or hunt with the other boys, but had to do all of the hard work. Whenever the camp broke up the family always tried to steal away and leave the boy behind, but sooner or later he found their new camp and went to them because he had no other place to go.

One time several families went in boats to an island in a large lake to hunt eggs, and the orphan boy went with them. After they had filled their boats with eggs they secretly made ready to go back to the mainland. In the night, while the orphan boy was asleep, they stole away in their boats, leaving him to starve on the lonely island.

The boy wandered about the island, eating only the scraps that he could find around the dead camp fires, until he was almost starved. As he did not have a bow and arrows, he could not hunt, but he sat by the water's edge and tried to catch fish as they swam past him. One day as he sat on the lonely shore he saw a large animal with horns coming to him through the water. He sat very still and watched the

animal, for he was too frightened to run away. The monster
came straight to him, then raised his head out of the water
and said: "Boy, I have come to save you. I saw the people
desert you and I have taken pity upon you and come to
rescue you. Get upon my back and hold to my horns and I
will carry you to the mainland."

The boy was no longer afraid, but climbed upon the
animal's back. "Keep your eyes on the blue sky, and if you
see a star tell me at once," the animal said to him. They had
not gone far when the boy cried, "There in the west is a big
star." The monster looked up and saw the star, then turned
around at once and swam back to the island as fast as he
could. The next day he came and took the boy again, telling
him, as before, to call out the moment that he saw a star
appear in the sky. They had gone a little farther than they
had the day before when the boy cried out, "There in the
west is a star." The animal turned around and went to the
shore.

The next day and the next four days he started with the boy,
and each time he succeeded in getting a little farther before
the boy saw the star. The sixth time they were within a few
feet of the opposite shore when the boy saw the star. He
wanted to reach the shore so badly that he thought he
would keep still and not tell the monster that he saw the
star, for he knew that he would take him back to the island
at once if he did. He said nothing, and so the monster swam
on until they were almost in shallow water, when the boy
saw a great black cloud roll in front of the star. He became
frightened and jumped off of the animal's back and swam
to the shore.

Just as he jumped something struck the animal with an
awful crash and he rolled over dead. When the boy came
upon the shore a handsome young man came up to him and

said: "You have done me a great favor. For a long time I have tried to kill this monster, because he makes the water of the lake dangerous, but until now I could never get the chance. In return for what you have done, I will take you with me to the sky, if you care to go." The boy said that he wanted to go, as he was alone and friendless upon the earth. The man, who was Evening-Star, took him with him to the sky, and there he may be seen as Orphan-Star who stands near Evening-Star.

Tale of the Girl Who Had Power to Call the Buffalo

Dorsey, George A. Traditions of the Caddo. Washington: Carnegie Institution. 1905.

A girl who had power to call the buffalo lived with her six brothers. The brothers were stars, and every night they left the girl to travel through the sky. Every morning after they had returned from their nightly journey they put the girl in a swing of lariat rope that hung down from the sky and swung her through the air. As she swung through the air the buffalo saw her and came. The boys killed all that they wanted, and then the rest of the herd went away. In this way the girl called the buffalo for her brothers, and so they always had plenty to eat.

One time Coyote came to visit them, and, finding that they always had meat, he decided to come and live with them. The brothers did not think much of Coyote, but they decided to let him stay. Every morning he watched the boys put their sister in the swing and swing her until the buffalo came. Before the brothers would let Coyote watch them swing her they made him promise that he would never try to do the same while they were gone, because if any one else tried to swing the girl he would swing her too hard and she would swing to the sky and never return. Coyote promised, but one day while all of the brothers were gone he called the girl to come and get into the swing. She refused, but he threatened her and made her obey him. She climbed into the swing and Coyote pushed her. The buffalo did not come, and so he pushed her again and caused her to go higher and higher through the air until she disappeared. Coyote became frightened and called to her to come down, saying that if she did not come he would jump up and pull her down. The girl did not come, and he could not see her.

When the brothers came home they missed their sister and asked Coyote where she was. He said that he did not know, but that he thought some monster had carried her away. The brothers knew that Coyote had lied, and that he had been the cause of her disappearance. They drove Coyote away, telling him that he and his children would always be hungry because he had disobeyed them. Then they held a council among themselves and decided to go to the sky and live there with their sister.

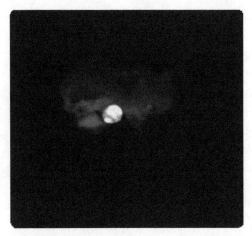

The Man Who Married the Moon

Isleta Pueblo
Published by
Charles F. Lummis
in St. Nicholas
Magazine in 1897.

Long before the first Spaniards came to New Mexico, Isleta stood where it stands today--on a lava ridge that defies the gnawing current of the Rio Grande. In those far days, Nah-chu-ru-chu, "The Bluish Light of Dawn," dwelt in Isleta, and was a leader of his people. A weaver by trade, his rude loom hung from the dark rafters of his room; and in it he wove the strong black mantas or robes like those which are the dress of Pueblo women to this day.

Besides being very wise in medicine, Nah-chu-ru-chu was young, and tall, and strong, and handsome. All the girls of the village thought it a shame that he did not care to take a wife. For him the shyest dimples played, for him the whitest teeth flashed out, as the owners passed him in the plaza; but he had no eyes for them. Then, in the custom of the Tiwa, bashful fingers worked wondrous fringed shirts of buckskin, or gay awl sheaths, which found their way to his house by unknown messengers.

But Nah-chu-ru-chu paid no more attention to the gifts than to the smiles, and just kept weaving and weaving such mantas as were never seen in the land of the Tee-wahn before or since.

Two of his admirers were sisters who were called, in Tiwa
language, Ee-eh-ch-choo-ri-ch'ahm-n- the Yellow Corn
Maidens. They were both young and pretty, but they "had
the evil road," or were witches, possessed of a magic power
which they always used for ill. When all the other girls
gave up, discouraged at Nah-chu-ru-shu's indifference, the
Yellow Corn Maidens kept coming day after day, trying to
win his notice. At last the matter became so annoying to
Nah-chu-ru-chu that he hired the deep-voiced town crier to
go through all the streets and announce that in four days
Nah-chu-ru-chu would choose a wife.

For dippers to take water from the big earthen jars, the
Tiwa used then, as they use to-day, queer little omates
made of a gourd. But Nahchu-ru-chu, being a great
medicine man and very rich, had a dipper of pure pearl,
shaped like the gourds, but wonderfully precious.

"On the fourth day," proclaimed the crier, "Nah-chu-ru-chu
will hang his pearl omate at his door, when every girl who
will may throw a handful of cornmeal at it. And she whose
meal is so well ground that it sticks to the omate, she shall
be the wife of Nah-chu-ru-chu!"

When this strange news came rolling down the still evening
air, there was a great scampering of little moccasined feet.
The girls ran out from hundreds of gray adobe houses to
catch every word; and when the crier had passed on, they
ran back into the storerooms and began to ransack the corn
bins for the biggest, evenest, and most perfect ears.
Shelling the choicest, each took her few handfuls of kernels
to the sloping metate, and with the mano, or hand stone,
scrubbed the blue grist up and down and up and down till
the hard corn was a soft blue meal. All the next day, and
the next, and the next, they ground it over and over again,
until it grew finer than ever flour was before; and every girl
felt sure that her meal would stick to the omate of the

handsome young weaver. The Yellow Corn Maidens
worked hardest of all; day and night for four days they
ground and ground, with all the magic spells they knew.

Now, in those far-off days the moon had not gone into the
sky to live, but was a maiden of Isleta. And a very beautiful
girl she was, but blind of one eye. She had long admired
Nah-chu-ru-chu, but was always too maidenly to try to
attract his attention as the other girls had done; and at the
time when the crier made his proclamation, she happened
to be away at her father's ranch. It was only upon the fourth
day that she returned to town, and in a few moments the
girls were to go with their meal to test it upon the magic
dipper. The two Yellow Corn Maidens were just coming
from their house as she passed, and they told her what was
to be done. They were very confident of success, and hoped
to pain her. They laughed derisively as she went running to
her home.

By this time a long file of girls was coming to Nah-chu-ru-
chu's house, outside whose door hung the pearl omate.
Each girl carried in her hand a little jar of meal. As they
passed the door, one by one, each took from the jar a
handful and threw it against the magic dipper. But each
time the meal dropped to the ground, and left the pure pearl
undimmed and radiant as ever.

At last came the Yellow Corn Maidens, who had waited to
watch the failure of the others. As they came where they
could see Nah-chu-ru-chu sitting at his loom, they called:
"Ah! Here we have the meal that will stick!" and each
threw a handful at the omate. But it did not stick at all; and
still from his seat Nah-chu-ru-chu could see, in the shell's
mirror like surface, all that went on outside.

The Yellow Corn Maidens were very angry, and instead of
passing on as the others had done, they stood there and kept

throwing and throwing at the omate, which smiled back at them with undiminished luster.

Just then, last of all, came the moon, with a single handful of meal which she had hastily ground. The two sisters were in a fine rage by this time, and mocked her, saying:

"Hoh! Pah-hlee-oh, Moon, you poor thing, we are very sorry for you! Here we have been grinding our meal for four days and still it will not stick, and we did not tell you till today. How then can you ever hope to win Nah-chu-ru-chu? Puh, you silly little thing!"

But the moon paid no attention whatsoever to their taunts. Drawing back her little dimpled hand, she threw the meal gently against the pearl omate, and so fine was it ground that every tiniest bit of it clung to the polished shell, and not a particle fell to the ground!

When Nah-chu-ru-chu saw that, he rose up quickly from his loom and came and took the moon by the hand, saying: "You are she who shall be my wife. You shall never want for anything, since I have very much." And he gave her many beautiful mantas, and cotton wraps, and fat boots of buckskin that wrap round and round, that she might dress as the wife of a rich chief. But the Yellow Corn Maidens, who had seen it all, went away vowing vengeance on the moon.

Nah-chu-ru-chu and his sweet moon-wife were very happy together. There was no other such housekeeper in all the pueblo as she, and no other hunter brought home so much buffalo meat from the vast plains to the east, nor so many antelopes, and black-tailed deer, and jack rabbits from the Manzanos, as did Nah-chu-ru-chu. But constantly he was saying to her:

"Moon-wife, beware of the Yellow Corn Maidens, for they have the evil road and will try to do you harm; but you must always refuse to do whatever they propose."

And always the young wife promised.

One day the Yellow Corn Maidens came to the house and said: "Friend Nah-chu-ru-chu, we are going to the llano, the plain, to gather amole." (Amole is a soapy root the Pueblos use for washing.) "Will you not let your wife go with us?"

"Oh, yes, she may go," said Nah-chu-ru-chu. But taking her aside, he said: "Now be sure that while you are with them, you refuse whatever they may propose."

The moon promised, and started away with the Yellow Corn Maidens.

In those days there was only a thick forest of cottonwoods where now the smiling vineyards, gardens, and orchards of Isleta are spread, and to reach the llano the three women had to go through the forest. In the very center of it they came to a deep pozo-a square well, with steps at one side leading down to the water's edge.

"Ay!" said the Yellow Corn Maidens, "How hot and thirsty is our walk! Come, let us get a drink of water."

But the moon, remembering her husband's words, said politely that she did not wish to drink. They urged in vain, but at last, looking down into the pozo, they called:

Oh, moon-friend, moon-friend! Come and look in this still water, and see how pretty you are!"

The moon, you must know, has always been just as fond of looking at herself in the water as she is to this very day; and forgetting Nahchu-ru-chu's warning, she came to the brink and looked down upon her fair reflection. But at that very moment the two witch sisters pushed her head foremost into the pozo, and drowned her; and then they filled the well with earth, and went away as happy as wicked hearts can be.

As the sun crept along the adobe floor, closer and closer to his seat, Nah-chu-ru-chu began to look oftener from his loom to the door. When the shadows were very long, he sprang suddenly to his feet, and walked to the house of the Yellow Corn Maidens with long, long strides.

"Yellow Corn Maidens," he asked them very sternly, "where is my little wife?" "Why, isn't she at home?" asked the wicked sisters, as if greatly surprised. "She got enough amole long before we did." "Ah," groaned Nah-chu-ru-chu within himself, "it is as I thought they have done her ill."

But without a word to them he turned on his heel and went away.

From that hour all went wrong at Isleta; for Nah-chu-ru-chu held the well-being of all his people, even unto life and death. Paying no attention to what was going on about him, he sat motionless upon the topmost crosspiece of the estufa (the kiva, or sacred council chamber ladder the highest point in all the town) with his head bowed upon his hands. There he sat for days, never speaking, never moving. The children who played along the streets looked up with awe to the motionless figure, and ceased their boisterous play. The old men shook their heads gravely, and muttered: 'We are in evil times, for Nah-chu-ru-chu is mourning, and will not be comforted; and there is no more rain, so that our crops are dying in the fields. What shall we do?"

At last all the councilors met together, and decided that there must be another effort made to find the lost wife. It was true that the great Nah-chu-ru-chu had searched for her in vain, and the people had helped him; but perhaps someone else might be more fortunate. So they took some of the sacred smoking weed wrapped in a corn husk and went to the eagle, who has the sharpest eyes in all the world. Giving him the sacred gift, they said:

"Eagle-friend, we see Nah-chu-ru-chu in great trouble, for he has lost his moon-wife. Come, search for her, we pray you, to discover if she be alive or dead."

So the eagle took the offering, and smoked the smoke prayer; and then he went winging upward into the sky. Higher and higher he rose, in great upward circles, while his keen eyes noted every stick, and stone, and animal on the face of all the world. But with all his eyes, he could see nothing of the lost wife; and at last he came back sadly, and said:

"People-friends, I went up to where I could see the whole world, but I could not find her."

Then the people went with an offering to the coyote, whose nose is sharpest in all the world, and besought him to try and find the moon. The coyote smoked the smoke prayer, and started off with his nose to the ground, trying to find her tracks. He trotted all over the earth; but at last he too came back without finding what he sought.

Then the troubled people got the badger to search, for he is the best of all the beasts at digging (it was he whom the Trues employed to dig the caves in which the people first dwelt when they came to this world). The badger trotted and pawed, and dug everywhere, but he could not find the moon; and he came home very sad.

Then they asked the osprey, who can see furthest under water, and he sailed high above the lakes and rivers in the world, till he could count the pebbles and the fish in them, but he too failed to discover the lost moon.

By this time the crops were dead and sere in the fields, and thirsty animals walked crying along the river. Scarcely could the people themselves dig deep enough to find water to keep them alive. They were at a loss, but at last they thought: We will go now to the P'ah-ku-ee-teh-aydeh (the water-goose grandfather, which means turkey buzzard), who can find the dead-for surely she is dead, or the others would have found her.

So they went to him, and besought him. The turkey buzzard wept when he saw Nah-chu-ru-chu still sitting there upon the ladder, and said: "Truly it is sad for our great friend; but for me, I am afraid to go, since they who are more mighty than I have already failed. Yet I will try." And spreading his broad wings, he went climbing up the spiral ladder of the sky. Higher he wheeled, and higher, till at last not even the eagle could see him. Up and up, till the sun began to singe his head, and not even the eagle had ever been so high. He cried with pain, but still he kept mounting-until he was so close to the sun that all the feathers were burned from his head and neck. But he could see nothing, and at last, frantic with the burning, he came wheeling downward. When he got back to the estufa where all the people were waiting, they saw that his head and neck had been burned bare of feathers-and from that day to this the feathers would never grow out again.

"And did you see nothing?" they all asked, when they had bathed his burns.

"Nothing," he answered, "except that when I was halfway down, I saw in the middle of yon cottonwood forest a little mound covered with all the beautiful flowers in the world."

"Oh!" cried Nah-chu-ru-chu, speaking for the first time, "Go, friend, and bring me one flower from the very middle of the mound."

Off flew the buzzard, and in a few minutes returned with a little white flower. Nah-chu-ru-chu took it and, descending from the ladder in silence, walked solemnly to his house, while all the wondering people followed.

When Nah-chu-ru-chu came inside his home once more, he took a new manta and spread it in the middle of the room. Laying the wee white flower tenderly in its center, he put another manta above it. Then, dressing himself in the splendid buckskin suit that the lost wife had made him, and taking in his right hand the sacred guaje, rattle, he seated himself at the head of the mantas and sang:

"Shu-nah, shu-nah! Ai-ay, ai-ay, ai-ay-ay. Seeking her, seeking her! There-away, there-away."

When he had finished the song, all could see that the flower had begun to grow, so that it lifted the upper manta a little. Again he sang, shaking his gourd; and still the flower kept growing.

Again and again he sang; and when he had finished for the fourth time, it was plain to all that a human form lay between the two mantas. And when he sang his song the fifth time, the form sat up and moved. Tenderly he lifted away the upper cloth; and there sat his sweet moon-wife, fairer than ever, and alive as before!

For four days the people danced and sang in the public square. Nahchu-ru-chu was happy again; and now the rain began to fall. The choked earth drank and was glad and green, and the dead crops came to life.

When his wife told him what the witch sisters had done, he was very angry; and that day he made a beautiful hoop to play the hoop game. He painted it, and put many strings across it, and decorated it with beaded buckskin.

"Now," said he, "the wicked Yellow Corn Maidens will come to congratulate you, and will pretend not to know where you were. You must not speak of that, but invite them to go out and play a game with you."

In a day or two the witch sisters did come, with deceitful words; and the moon invited them to go out and play a game. They went up to the edge of the llano, and there she let them get a glimpse of the pretty hoop.

"Oh, give us that, moon-friend," they teased. But she refused. At last, however, she said: "Well, we will play the hoop game. I will stand here, and you there; and if, when I roll it to you, you catch it before it falls upon its side, you may have it."

So the witch sisters stood a little way down the hill, and she rolled the bright hoop. As it came trundling to them, both grasped it at the same instant; and lo! instead of the Yellow Corn Maidens, there were two great snakes, with tears rolling down ugly faces. The moon came and put upon their heads a little of the pollen of the corn blossom (still used by Pueblo snake charmers) to tame them, and a pinch of sacred meal for their food.

"Now," she said, "you have the reward of treacherous friends. Here shall be your home among these rocks and cliffs forever, but you must never be found upon the prairie; and you must never bite a person. Remember you are women, and must be gentle."

And then the moon went home to her husband, and they were very happy together. As for the sister snakes, they still dwell where she bade them, and never venture away; though sometimes the people bring them to their houses to catch mice, for these snakes never hurt a person.

Tales of the Girl Who Married a Star

Dorsey, George A. Traditions of the Caddo. Washington: Carnegie Institution. 1905.

One time a maiden slept in an arbor, and as she lay under the blue sky she watched the stars. One star especially she watched, and she wished that it would become a man and marry her, for she did not care for any of the young men of the village. She went to sleep wishing that the star would marry her.

When she awoke she saw no stars, but an old man sitting by the fireside. "Where am I?" she asked. "Your wish is granted; you are the Star's wife. I am the Star." She began to cry, for the man was old and homely and she was young and beautiful, and so she had dreamed that her husband would be. The Star's sister was preparing something to eat, and she told the girl to stop crying and come and eat.

After a while the two women went out to dig potatoes. They saw one big potato, and the girl asked the Star's sister what the big potato was for. She answered that it was the door of heaven, and that it covered the entrance to the world beneath. Then the girl cried again and begged the woman to let her go back to her people. She told her how unhappy she was and what a mistake she had made in wishing to marry the Star.

The woman told the Star all that his wife had said, and so the Star agreed to let her return to her people in six days. The two women went out to gather bark from young elm trees to make a rope for the girl to climb down to earth on. After they had gathered the bark they began to make the rope and the Star helped them.

After six days the rope was only half long enough, and so the old man said she would have to wait six more days until they could complete the rope. On the eleventh day the rope was finished, and the Star's sister cooked some corn meal for the girl to eat on the way and filled a squash vessel with water for her.

The Star told her to start early the next morning, for it would take her ten winters and summers to get to the earth. They fastened her to the end of the rope and then removed the potato and let her through the hole and gradually let the rope slip out. At first she could see nothing but darkness; then after a long time she could see the earth. After she had traveled through many waves of warm and cold air, she knew she had been on her way many summers and winters. Her food was almost gone and still she was a long way from the earth.

Suddenly the rope ceased to slip and she hung swinging back and forth. She had come to the end of the rope. It was not long enough. She hung there for a long time and was about to die from hunger and weariness when she saw Buzzard circling around below her.

She called to Buzzard to come and help her. He came, and after she had told him her story he told her to get on his

back; that he would take her down to earth. Buzzard flew
for a long time and the girl was heavy, so that he nearly
gave out. He saw Hawk flying below him, and he called
Hawk and asked him to help him take the girl home. Hawk
flew with the girl until they could see the mountains and
the rivers; then he gave out.

Buzzard took the girl on his back again, and thanking
Hawk for his help, told him to go his way; that he could
take the girl on to her home. Buzzard flew on and on until
they could see the trees, and soon they were even with the
tops of the highest trees. Then Buzzard told the girl to go
into her lodge when she went home and not to let any one
but her father and mother see her. She was so thin that she
was little more than skin and bones. Buzzard flew to the
ground and lighted very gently just outside the girl's
village. He pointed out her parents' lodge to her and then
said good-bye and flew away.

The girl rested for a while and then began to walk very
slowly to the lodge, for she was weak and exhausted. On
the way she saw a woman coming toward her. She hid
behind a bush, but the woman saw her and screamed, for
the girl was so thin that she frightened her. The girl told the
woman not to be afraid and told her who she was. Then the
woman recognized the lost maiden and helped her to her
lodge.

Her mother did not know her at first, but when she found
that the girl was her daughter she threw her arms about her
and wept. The news of the girl's return spread throughout
the village, but her parents obeyed her wish and refused to
let any one see her until after the tenth day. Then they came
to her tipi and she told them her story and especially about
the kindness shown her by Buzzard.

After that the people always left one buffalo for the buzzards after a big killing.

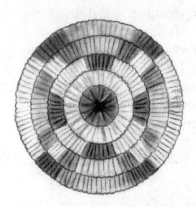

The Two War Gods and the Two Maidens

A Hopi Legend
H. R. Voth, The
Traditions of the Hopi,
Field Columbian
Museum
Anthropological Series,
1905

A long time ago Pöokónghoya and his little brother Balö'ngahoya lived north of the village at the shrine of the Achámali. One day they heard that two beautiful maidens were watching some fields west of the village of Hû'ckovi, of which the ruins may still be seen a few miles north-west of Oraíbi. They concluded that they would go hunting and at the same time visit those two maidens.

When they arrived there the maidens joyfully greeted them and they were joking and teasing each other. The maidens believed that the two brothers had come with the intention to marry them, and they said, in a half-jesting manner, to their suitors: "We will cut off an arm from each one of you, and if you do not die you may own us."

The younger brother was at once willing, saying to his elder brother: "They are beautiful; let us not be afraid of having our arm cut off." The elder brother hesitated, saying, that that would hurt. So the younger brother said, "I am willing," laid his right arm over the edge of the mealing trough at which the maidens had been working, and one of the maidens struck the arm with the upper mealing stone and cut it off, the arm dropping into the trough or bin. His elder brother hereupon laid his arm over the edge of the

bin, which consisted of a thin, sharp slab, and the other
maiden also cut his arm off with her mealing stone. Now
the two brothers said: "If we recover, we shall come after
you. Hand us our arm, now." The maidens did so and the
two brothers left, each one carrying his severed arm,
arriving at their home north of Oraíbi, they told their
grandmother what had happened.

"There," she said, "you have been in something again and
have done some mischief."

"Yes," they said, "We met two beautiful maidens and liked
them very much, and so we allowed them to cut off our
arms. "Very well, she said, "I am going to set you right
again." So she asked them to lay down north of the
fireplace.

She placed the two arms by their sides, covered them up,
whereupon she commenced to sing a song. When she was
through singing, she told them now to get up. They did so
and found their arms healed. The next day they proceeded
to the house of the maidens, who were surprised to see
them fully recovered. The older of the two sisters was the
prettier one and Pöokónghoya wanted to choose that one.
His younger brother protested, saying: "Yesterday you
were not willing to have your arm cut off, as you were then
afraid, and now you want to have the first choice. I had my
arm cut off first and I am going to choose first," to which
his elder brother finally consented. They slept with the
maidens that night and then left them and returned to their
home north of Oraíbi.

The Man in the Moon

*A Lillooet Legend
Teit, Journal of
American Folk-
Lore, xxv, 298, No.
3*

The three Frog sisters had a house in a swamp, where they lived together. Not very far away lived a number of people in another house. Among them were Snake and Beaver, who were friends.

They were well-grown lads, and wished to marry the Frog girls.

One-night Snake went to Frog's house, and, crawling up to one of the sisters, put his hand on her face. She awoke, and asked him who he was. Learning that he was Snake, she said she would not marry him, and told him to leave at once. She called him hard names, such as, "slimy-fellow," "small-eyes," etc. Snake returned, and told his friend of his failure.

Next night Beaver went to try, and, crawling up to one of the sisters, he put his hand on her face. She awoke, and, finding out who he was, she told him to be gone. She called him names, such as, "short-legs," "big-belly," "big-buttocks." Beaver felt hurt, and, going home, began to cry. His father asked him what the matter was, and the boy told him. He said, "That is nothing. Don't cry! It will rain too much." But young Beaver said, "I will cry."

As he continued to cry, much rain fell, and soon the swamp where the Frogs lived was flooded. Their house was under the water, which covered the tops of the tall swamp-grass. The Frogs got cold, and went to Beaver's house, and said to him, "We wish to marry your sons." But old Beaver said, "No! You called us hard names."

The water was now running in a regular stream. So the Frogs swam away downstream until they reached a whirlpool, which sucked them in, and they descended to the house of the Moon. The latter invited them to warm themselves at the fire; but they said, "No. We do not wish to sit by the fire. We wish to sit there," pointing at him.

He said, "Here?" at the same time pointing at his feet. They said, "No, not there." Then he pointed to one part of his body after another, until he reached his brow. When he said, "Will you sit here?" they all cried out, "Yes," and jumped on his face, thus spoiling his beauty. The Frog's sisters may be seen on the moon's face at the present day.

Tale of the Girl Who Married a Star 2

Dorsey, George A. Traditions of the Caddo. Washington: Carnegie Institution. 1905.

Long ago there lived a large family–father, mother, and eight children, four girls and four boys. They were all beautiful children, especially one of the girls, who was exceptionally beautiful.

The time came when three of the girls were married, but the youngest and most beautiful would not receive the attention of any one. The girl was peculiar in her tastes and roamed around alone. She wished to go away somewhere, for she was tired of her home.

One time while she was walking alone she began praying to the spirits to help her, that she might go wherever she wished. That night she was outside the lodge watching the stars, and she found that the stars were not all alike; that some were bright and some were very dim. Finally she saw one, the North Star, that was very bright, and then again she began to pray to the spirits to help her, and she wished that she might marry the star and become his wife.

She ceased praying and did not know where she was for a while, and the first thing she saw was a very old man sitting by the fireside with his head down. She stood for a long

while watching him. At first she could not believe herself,
and she thought that she was only dreaming, but finally the
old man looked up at her and said: "You are the young
woman who wished to marry me and you have your wish;
you are now in my home as my wife, as you wished." She
did not like the looks of the old man, and she wished that
she might get away from him; but her wish was not granted
and she had to stay.

She tried many ways to get away, but all failed, and she
was about to give up when she thought of a great big round
stone that the Star had told her not to move, for it was very
dangerous to move it. One time when the Star was away on
a visit she thought she would go over and lift the stone and
see what was there. She lifted the stone and found that she
could look clear down to the earth, and then she began to
wonder how she could get down to the earth.

She put the stone back in its place, and when the Star came
back he asked her where she had been, and she told him
that she had been at home all the time. When night came
she went to bed, and as she was wondering how to get
down to the earth she thought about making a long rope out
of soapweeds, for she had heard the old story about the
people making such a rope long ago.

When the Star went away for his nightly trip she would go
out and cut soapweeds; but when he came back he would
always find her at home, and so he never thought of her
doing anything of the kind. Finally she had enough weeds
cut, and then she began to make the rope. It took her a long
while before she had the rope finished.

One day she thought she had rope enough to reach down to
the earth. She went and lifted the stone to one side and
dropped the rope down just as fast as she could. She finally

came to the end of the rope; then she fastened it to the rock and placed the rock over the hole again and went back home. When the man came she was at home, but the next time he went away she went to the hole and began to climb down.

It took her a long while before she could see the land plainly, and before she came to the tops of the trees she came to the end of the rope, and she did not know what to do. She was getting very tired, but she hung there for some time, and after a while she heard a noise near her and she looked and saw a bird. The bird passed under her feet several times, and when he passed the fourth time he told her that he would take her down and carry her home if she would step on to his back.

She stepped on the bird's back, and he asked her if she was ready, and she said that she was; then he told her to let go of the rope. She did so, and the bird began to fly downward very easily. The bird asked if she would let him take her on to her home, and she said that she would. The bird then took her to her home, and when they came near, the bird let her down and told her that he had to go back to his home; but before leaving her he told her that he was Black Eagle.

Children of the Sun

Osage
From Alice Fletcher and Francis Lafleche, who recorded this myth in 1911.

Way beyond the earth, a part of the Osage lived in the sky. They wanted to know where they came from, so they went to the sun. He told them that they were his children. Then they wandered still farther and came to the moon. She told them that she gave birth to them, and that the sun was their father. She said that they must leave the sky and go down to live on earth. They obeyed, but found the earth covered with water. They could not return to their home in the sky, so they wept and called out, but no answer came from anywhere. They floated about in the air, seeking in every direction for help from some god; but they found none.

The animals were with them, and of these the elk inspired all creatures with confidence because he was the finest and most stately. The Osage appealed to the elk for help, and he dropped into the water and began to sink. Then he called to the winds, and they came from all quarters and blew until the waters went upward in mist.

At first only rocks were exposed, and the people traveled on the rocky places that produced no plants to eat. Then the waters began to go down until the soft earth was exposed.

When this happened, the elk in his joy rolled over and over, and all his loose hairs clung to the soil. The hairs grew, and from them sprang beans, corn, potatoes, and wild turnips, and then all the grasses and trees.

The Woman Who Fell from the Sky

Seneca
From Stith Thompson, Tales of the North American Indians
(1929)

A long time ago human beings lived high up in what is now
called heaven. They had a great and illustrious chief.

It so happened that this chief's daughter was taken very ill
with some strange affliction. Every known remedy was
tried in an attempt to cure her, but none had any effect.

Near the lodge of this chief stood a great tree, which every
year bore corn used for food. One of the friends of the chief
had a dream in which he was advised to tell the chief that,
in order to cure his daughter, he must lay her beside this
tree, and that he must have the tree dug up. This advice was
carried out to the letter. While the people were at work and
the young woman lay there, a young man came along. He
was very angry and said: "It is not at all right to destroy this
tree. Its fruit is all that we have to live on." With this
remark he gave the young woman who lay there ill a shove
with his foot, causing her to fall into the hole that had been
dug.

Now, that hole opened into this world, which was then all water, on which floated waterfowl of many kinds. There was no land at that time. It came to pass that as these waterfowl saw this young woman falling they shouted, "Let us receive her," whereupon they, at least some of them, joined their bodies together, and the young woman fell on this platform of bodies. When these were wearied they asked, "Who will volunteer to care for this woman?"

The great Turtle then took her, and when he got tired of holding her, he in turn asked who would take his place. At last the question arose as to what they should do to provide her with a permanent resting place in this world. Finally it was decided to prepare the earth, on which she would live in the future. To do this it was determined that soil from the bottom of the primal sea should be brought up and placed on the broad, firm carapace of the Turtle, where it would increase in size to such an extent that it would accommodate all the creatures that should be produced thereafter. After much discussion the toad was finally persuaded to dive to the bottom of the waters in search of soil. Bravely making the attempt, he succeeded in bringing up soil from the depths of the sea. This was carefully spread over the carapace of the Turtle, and at once both began to grow in size and depth.

After the young woman recovered from the illness from which she suffered when she was cast down from the upper world, she built herself a shelter, in which she lived quite contentedly. In the course of time she brought forth a girl baby, who grew rapidly in size and intelligence.

When the daughter had grown to young womanhood, the mother and she were accustomed to go out to dig wild potatoes. Her mother had said to her that in doing this she must face the west at all times. Before long the young daughter gave signs that she was about to become a mother. Her mother reproved her, saying that she had violated the injunction not to face the east, as her condition showed that she had faced the wrong way while digging potatoes. It is said that the breath of the West Wind had entered her person, causing conception. When the days of her delivery were at hand, she overheard twins within her body in a hot debate as to which should be born first and as to the proper place of exit, one declaring that he was going to emerge through the armpit of his mother, the other saying that he would emerge in the natural way. The first one born, who was of a reddish color, was called Othagwenda, that is, Flint. The other, who was light in color, was called Djuskaha, that is, the Little Sprout.

The grandmother of the twins liked Djuskaha [Little Sprout] and hated the other, so they cast Othagwenda [Flint] into a hollow tree some distance from the lodge.

The boy who remained in the lodge grew very rapidly, and soon was able to make himself bows and arrows and to go out to hunt in the vicinity. Finally, for several days he returned home without his bow and arrows. At last he was asked why he had to have a new bow and arrows every morning. He replied that there was a young boy in a hollow tree in the area who used them. The grandmother inquired where the tree stood, and he told her; whereupon then they went there and brought the other boy home again.

When the boys had grown to man's estate, they decided that it was necessary for them to increase the size of their island, so they agreed to start out together, afterward separating to create forests and lakes and other things. They parted as agreed, Othagwenda [Flint] going westward and Djuskaha [Little Sprout] eastward. In the course of time, on returning they met in their shelter or lodge at night, then agreeing to go the next day to see what each had made.

First they went west to see what Othagwenda [Flint] had made. It was found that he had made the country all rocks and full of ledges, and also a mosquito that was very large. Djuskaha asked the mosquito to run, in order that he might see whether the insect could fight. The mosquito ran, and sticking his bill through a sapling, thereby made it fall, at which Djuskaha [Little Sprout] said, "That will not be right, for you would kill the people who are about to come." So, seizing him, he rubbed him down in his hands, causing him to become very small; then he blew on the mosquito, whereupon he flew away. He also modified some of the other animals that his brother had made. After returning to their lodge, they agreed to go the next day to see what Djuskaha [Little Sprout] had fashioned.

On visiting the east the next day, they found that Djuskaha had made a large number of animals which were so fat that they could hardly move; that he had made the sugar-maple trees to drop syrup; that he had made the sycamore tree to bear fine fruit; that the rivers were so formed that half the water flowed upstream and the other half downstream. Then the reddish-colored brother, Othagwenda [Flint], was greatly displeased with what his brother had made, saying that the people who were about to come would live too easily and be too happy. So he shook violently the various animals--the bears, deer, and turkeys--causing them to become small at once, a characteristic that attached itself to their descendants. He also caused the sugar maple to drop sweetened water only, and the fruit of the sycamore to become small and useless; and lastly he caused the water of the rivers to flow in only one direction, because the original plan would make it too easy for the human beings who were about to come to navigate the streams.

The inspection of each other's work resulted in a deadly disagreement between the brothers, who finally came to grips and blows, and Othagwenda [Flint] was killed in the fierce struggle.

Sun Sister and Moon Brother

Inuit
Eskimo: Boas,
Report of the
Bureau of
American
Ethnology, VI, 597

In olden times a brother and his sister lived in a large village in which there was a singing house, and every night the sister with her playfellows enjoyed themselves in this house. Once upon a time, when all the lamps in the singing house were extinguished, somebody came in and outraged her. She was unable to recognize him; but she blackened her hands with soot and when the same again happened besmeared the man's back with it. When the lamps were re-lighted she saw that the violator was her brother. In great anger she sharpened a knife and cut off her breasts, which she offered to him, saying: "Since you seem to relish me, eat this." Her brother fell into a passion and she fled from him, running about the room. She seized a piece of wood (with which the lamps are kept in order) which was burning brightly and rushed out of the house. The brother took another one, but in his pursuit he fell down and extinguished his light, which continued to glow only faintly. Gradually both were lifted up and continued their course in the sky, the sister being transformed into the sun, the brother into the moon.

Whenever the new moon first appears she sings:

> Aningaga tapika, takirn tapika
> qaumidjatedlirpoq; qaumatitaudle.
> Aningaga tapika, tikipoq tapika.
>
> (My brother up there, the moon up there
> begins to shine; he will be bright.
> My brother up there, he is coming up there.)

Why the North Star Stands Still

Paiute

Long, long ago, when the world was young, the People of the Sky were so restless and travelled so much that they made trails in the heavens. Now, if we watch the sky all through the night, we can see which way they go.

But one star does not travel. That is the North Star. He cannot travel. He cannot move. When he was on the earth long, long ago, he was known as Na-gah, the mountain sheep, the son of Shinoh. He was brave, daring, sure-footed, and courageous. His father was so proud of him and loved him so much that he put large earrings on the sides of his head and made him look dignified, important, and commanding.

Every day, Na-gah was climbing, climbing, climbing. He hunted for the roughest and the highest mountains, climbed them, lived among them, and was happy. Once in the very long ago, he found a very high peak. Its sides were steep and smooth, and its sharp peak reached up into the clouds. Na-gah looked up and said, "I wonder what is up there. I will climb to the very highest point."

Around and around the mountain he travelled, looking for a trail. But he could find no trail. There was nothing but sheer cliffs all the way around. This was the first mountain Na-gah had ever seen that he could not climb.

He wondered and wondered what he should do. He felt sure
that his father would feel ashamed of him if he knew that
there was a mountain that his son could not climb. Na-gah
determined that he would find a way up to its top. His
father would be proud to see him standing on the top of
such a peak.

Again and again he walked around the mountain, stopping
now and then to peer up the steep cliff, hoping to see a
crevice on which he could find footing. Again and again, he
went up as far as he could, but always had to turn around
and come down. At last he found a big crack in a rock that
went down, not up. Down he went into it and soon found a
hole that turned upward. His heart was made glad. Up and
up he climbed.

Soon it became so dark that he could not see, and the cave
was full of loose rocks that slipped under his feet and rolled
down. Soon he heard a big, fearsome noise coming up
through the shaft at the same time the rolling rocks were
dashed to pieces at the bottom. In the darkness he slipped
often and skinned his knees. His courage and determination
began to fail. He had never before seen a place so dark and
dangerous. He was afraid, and he was also very tired.

"I will go back and look again for a better place to climb,"
he said to himself. "I am not afraid out on the open cliffs,
but this dark hole fills me with fear. I'm scared! I want to
get out of here!" But when Na-gah turned to go down, he
found that the rolling rocks had closed the cave below him.
He could not get down. He saw only one thing now that he
could do: He must go on climbing until he came out
somewhere.

After a long climb, he saw a little light, and he knew that he
was coming out of the hole. "Now I am happy," he said

aloud. "I am glad that I really came up through that dark hole."

Looking around him, he became almost breathless, for he found that he was on the top of a very high peak! There was scarcely room for him to turn around, and looking down from this height made him dizzy. He saw great cliffs below him, in every direction, and saw only a small place in which he could move. Nowhere on the outside could he get down, and the cave was closed on the inside..,

"Here I must stay until I die," he said. "But I have climbed my mountain! I have climbed my mountain at last!

He ate a little grass and drank a little water that he found in the holes in the rocks. Then he felt better. He was higher than any mountain he could see and he could look down on the earth, far below him.

About this time, his father was out walking over the sky. He looked everywhere for his son, but could not find him. He called loudly, "Na-gah! Na-gah!" And his son answered him from the top of the highest cliffs. When Shinoh saw him there, he felt sorrowful, to himself, "My brave son can never come down. Always he must stay on the top of the highest mountain. He can travel and climb no more.

"I will not let my brave son die. I will turn him into a star, and he can stand there and shine where everyone can see him. He shall be a guide mark for all the living things on the earth or in the sky."

And so Na-gah became a star that every living thing can see. It is the only star that will always be found at the same place. Always he stands still. Directions are set by him. Travelers, looking up at him, can always find their way. He does not move around as the other stars do, and so he is called "the Fixed Star." And because he is in the true north all the time, our people call him Qui-am-i Wintook Poot-see. These words mean "the North Star."

Besides Na-gah, other mountain sheep are in the sky. They are called "Big Dipper" and "Little Dipper." They too have found the great mountain and have been challenged by it. They have seen Na- gah standing on its top, and they want to go on up to him.

Shinoh, the father of North Star, turned them into stars, and you may see them in the sky at the foot of the big mountain. Always they are travelling. They go around and around the mountain, seeking the trail that leads upward to Na-gah, who stands on the top. He is still the North Star.

Eagle Boy
A Zuni Legend

Long ago, a boy was out walking one day when he found a young eagle that had fallen from its nest. He picked that eagle up and brought it home and began to care for it. He made a place for it to stay, and each day he went out and hunted for rabbits and other small game to feed it.

His mother asked him why he no longer came to work in the fields and help his family. "I must hunt for this eagle," the boy said. So it went on for a long time and the eagle grew large and strong as the boy hunted and fed it. Now it was large and strong enough to fly away if it wished to. But the eagle, stayed with the boy who had cared for it so well.

The boy's brothers criticized him for not doing his share of
work in the corn and melon fields, but Eagle Boy as they
now called him did not hear them. He cared only for his
bird. Even the boy's father, who was an important man in
the village, began to scold him for not helping. But still the
boy did not listen. So it was that the boy's brothers and his
older male relatives in his family came together and
decided that they must kill the eagle. They decided to do so
when they returned from the fields the following day.

When Eagle Boy came to his bird's cage, he saw that the
bird sat there with its head hanging down. He placed a
rabbit he had caught in the cage, but the eagle did not move
or eat it. "What is wrong, my eagle friend?" asked the boy.
Then the eagle spoke, he had never spoken to the boy
before. He said, "My friend, I cannot eat for I am filled
with sadness and sorrow." "But why are you so troubled?"
asked the boy. "It is because of you," said the eagle. You
have not done your work in the fields. Instead, you have
spent all of your time caring for me. Now your brothers and
family have decided to kill me so that you again will return
to your duties in the village. I have stayed here all of this
time because I have learned to love you. But now I must
leave. When the sun rises tomorrow, I will fly away and
never come back." "My eagle," said the boy, "I do not want
to stay here without you. You must take me with you." "My
friend, I cannot take you with me," You would not be able
to find your way through the sky. You would not be able to
eat raw food." said the eagle. "If you are certain, then you
may come with me. But you must do as I say. Come to me
at dawn, after the people have gone down to their fields.
Bring food to eat on our long journey across the sky. Put
food in pouches so you can sling them over your shoulders.
You must also bring two strings of bells and tie them to my
feet."

That night the boy filled the pouches with blue corn wafer
bread, dried meats and fruits. He made up two strings of
bells, tying them with strong rawhide. The next morning,
after the people had gone down to the fields, he went to the
eagle's cage and opened it. The eagle spread its wings wide.
"Now," he said to Eagle Boy, "tie the bells to my feet and
then climb onto my back and hold onto the base of my
wings." Eagle Boy climbed on and the eagle began to fly. It
rose higher and higher in slow circles above the village and
above the fields. The bells on the eagle's feet jingled and
the eagle sang and the boy sang with it:

Huli-i-i, hu-li-i-i-
Pa shish lakwa-a-a-a.........

So they sang and the people in the fields below heard them
singing, and they heard the sound of the bells Eagle Boy
had tied to the eagle's feet. They all looked up. "They are
leaving," the people called out in the village. "They are
leaving." Eagle Boy's parents yelled up to him, but he could
not hear them. The eagle and boy went higher and higher in
the sky until they were only a tiny speck and they
disappeared from the sight of the village people. The eagle
and the boy flew higher and higher until they came to an
opening in the clouds. They passed through and came out
into the Sky Land. They landed there on Turquoise
Mountain where the Eagle People lived.

Eagle Boy looked around the sky world. Everything was
smooth and white and clean clouds. "Here is my home," the
eagle said. He took the boy into the city in the sky, and
there were eagles all around them. They looked like people,
for they took off their wings and their clothing of feathers
when they were in their homes. The Eagle People made a
coat of feathers for the boy and taught him to wear it and to
fly. It took him a long time to learn, but soon he was able to

circle high above the land just like the Eagle People and he was an eagle himself. "You may fly anywhere," the old eagles told him, "anywhere except to the South. Never fly to the South Land."

All went well for Eagle Boy in his new life. One day, though, as he flew alone, he wondered what it was that was so terrible about the South. His curiosity grew, and he flew further and further toward the South. Lower and lower he flew and now he saw a beautiful city below with people dancing around red fires. "There is nothing to fear here," he said to himself, and flew lower still. Closer and closer he came, drawn by the red fires, until he landed. The people greeted him and drew him into the circle. He danced with them all night and then, when he grew tired, they gave him a place to sleep. When he woke the next morning and looked around, he saw the fires were gone. The houses no longer seemed bright and beautiful All around him there was dust, and in the dust there were bones. He looked for his cloak of eagle feathers, wanting to fly away from this city of the dead. But it was nowhere to be found. Then the bones rose up from the dust and came together. There were people made of bones all around him! He stood up and began to run away from them. The people made of bones chased him. Just as they were about to catch him, he saw a badger.

"Grandson," the badger said, "I will save you." Then the badger carried the boy down into his hole and the bone people could not follow. "You have been foolish," the badger scolded. "You did not listen to the warnings the eagles gave you. Now that you have been in this land in the South, they will not allow you to live with them anymore."

Then the badger took pity on Eagle Boy and showed him the way back to the city of the eagles. It was a long hard journey and when the boy reached the eagle city, he stood outside the high white walls. The eagles would not let him enter. "You have been to the South Land," they said. You can no longer live with us." At last, the eagle the boy had raised below took pity on him. After all, this boy had fed and cared for him. He brought the boy an old and ragged feather cloak. "With this cloak you may reach the home of your own people," he said. "But you can never return to our place in the sky." He gratefully accepted the gift of the tattered feather cloak. His flight back down to his people was a hard one, more difficult than any flights in Sky Land. He almost fell through the sky many times. His eagle friend circled and circled in the clouds watching over him. When he finally reached the village of his people on earth, the eagle flew down and carried off the feather cloak they had given him.

From that time on, Eagle Boy lived among his people. Though he lifted his eyes in joy whenever eagles soared overhead, he shared in the work in the fields, and his people were honored and happy to him among them. He could fly away if it wished to, but he the eagle stayed with the people who loved him.

The Wish to Marry a Star

An Ojibwa Legend
Speck, Memoirs of the
Geological Survey of Canada:
Anthropological Series, ix, 47

At the time of which my story speaks people were camping just as we are here. In the winter time they used birch bark wigwams. All the animals could then talk together.

Two girls, who were very foolish, talked foolishly and were in no respect like the other girls of their tribe, made their bed out-of-doors, and slept right out under the stars. The very fact that they slept outside during the winter proves how foolish they were.

One of these girls asked the other, "With what star would you like to sleep, the white one or the red one?" The other girl answered, "I'd like to sleep with the red star." "Oh, that's all right," said the first one, "I would like to sleep with the white star. He's the younger; the red is the older." Then the two girls fell asleep.

When they awoke, they found themselves in another world, the star world. There were four of them there, the two girls and the two stars who had become men. The white star was very, very old and was grey-headed, while the younger was red-headed. He was the red star. The girls stayed a long time in this star world, and the one who had chosen the white star was very sorry, for he was so old.

There was an old woman up in this world who sat over a

hole in the sky, and, whenever she moved, she showed them the hole and said, "That's where you came from." They looked down through and saw their people playing down below, and then the girls grew very sorry and very homesick. One evening, near sunset, the old woman moved a little way from the hole.

The younger girl heard the noise of the mitewin down below. When it was almost daylight, the old woman sat over the hole again and the noise of mitewin stopped; it was her spirit that made the noise. She was the guardian of the mitewin.

One morning the old woman told the girls, "If you want to go down where you came from, we will let you down, but get to work and gather roots to make a string-made rope, twisted. The two of you make coils of rope as high as your heads when you are sitting. Two coils will be enough." The girls worked for days until they had accomplished this.

They made plenty of rope and tied it to a big basket. They then got into the basket and the people of the star world lowered them down. They descended right into an Eagle's nest, but the people above thought the girls were on the ground and stopped lowering them. They were obliged to stay in the nest, because they could do nothing to help themselves.

Said one, "We'll have to stay here until some one comes to get us." Bear passed by. The girls cried out, "Bear, come and get us. You are going to get married sometime. Now is your chance!" Bear thought, "They are not very good-looking women." He pretended to climb up and then said, "I can't climb up any further."

And he went away, for the girls didn't suit him. Next came Lynx. The girls cried out again, "Lynx, come up and get us.

You will go after women some day!" Lynx answered, "I can't, for I have no claws," and he went away. Then an ugly-looking man, Wolverine, passed and the girls spoke to him. "Hey, wolverine, come and get us." Wolverine started to climb up, for he thought it a very fortunate thing to have these women and was very glad. When he reached them, they placed their hair ribbons in the nest.

Then Wolverine agreed to take one girl at a time, so he took the first one down and went back for the next. Then Wolverine went away with his two wives and enjoyed himself greatly, as he was ugly and nobody else would have him. They went far into the woods, and then they sat down and began to talk. "Oh!" cried one of the girls, "I forgot my hair ribbon." Then Wolverine said, "I will run back for it."

And he started off to get the hair ribbons. Then the girls hid and told the trees, whenever Wolverine should come back and whistle for them, to answer him by whistling. Wolverine soon returned and began to whistle for his wives, and the trees all around him whistled in answer. Wolverine, realizing that he had been tricked, gave up the search and departed very angry.

Old Man Above Creates the World

A Shasta Legend
Katharine Berry
Judson, Myths and
Legends of California
and the Old
Southwest, 1912

Long, long ago, when the world was so new that even the stars were dark, it was very, very flat.

Chareya, Old Man Above, could not see through the dark to the new, flat earth. Neither could he step down to it because it was so far below him.

With a large stone he bored a hole in the sky. Then through the hole he pushed down masses of ice and snow, until a great pyramid rose from the plain. Old Man Above climbed down through the hole he had made in the sky, stepping from cloud to cloud, until he could put his foot on top the mass of ice and snow.

Then with one long step he reached the earth.

The sun shone through the hole in the sky and began to melt the ice and snow. It made holes in the ice and snow. When it was soft, Chareya bored with his finger into the earth, here and there, and planted the first trees.

Streams from the melting snow watered the new trees and

made them grow. Then he gathered the leaves which fell from the trees and blew upon them. They became birds. He took a stick and broke it into pieces. Out of the small end he made fishes and placed them in the mountain streams.

Of the middle of the stick, he made all the animals except the grizzly bear. From the big end of the stick came the grizzly bear, who was made master of all. Grizzly was large and strong and cunning. When the earth was new he walked upon two feet and carried a large club. So strong was Grizzly that Old Man Above feared the creature he had made.

Therefore, so that he might be safe, Chareya hollowed out the pyramid of ice and snow as a tepee. There he lived for thousands of snows.

The Indians knew he lived there because they could see the smoke curling from the smoke hole of his tepee. When the pale-face came, Old Man Above went away. There is no longer any smoke from the smoke hole. White men call the tepee Mount Shasta.

The Nunne'hi and Other Spirit Folk
Cherokee

The Nûññë'hï or immortals, the "people who live anywhere," were a race of spirit people who lived in the highlands of the old Cherokee country and had a great many townhouses, especially in the bald mountains.

They had large townhouses in Pilot knob and under the old Nikwasi' mound in North Carolina, and another under Blood mountain, at the head of Nottely River, in Georgia. They were invisible excepting when they wanted to be seen, and then they looked and poke just like other Indians.

They were very fond of music and dancing, and hunters in the mountains would often hear the dance, songs and the drum beating in some invisible townhouse, but when they went toward the sound it would shift about and they would hear it behind them or away in some other direction, so that they could never find the place where the dance was.

They were a friendly people, too, and often brought lost
wanderers to their townhouses under the mountains and
cared for them there until they were rested and then guided
them back to their home . More than once, also, when the
Cherokee were hard pressed by the enemy, the Nûñnë'hï
warriors have come out, as they did at old Nikwasi', and
have saved them from defeat. Some people have thought
that they are the same as the Yûñwï Tsunsdi', the "Little
People"; but these are fairies, no larger in size than
children.

There was a man in Nottely town who had been with the
Nûñnë'hï when he was a boy, and he told Wafford all about
it. He was a truthful, hard-headed man, and Wafford had
heard the story so often from other people that he asked this
man to tell it. It was in this way:

When he was about 10 or 12 years old he was playing one
day near the river, shooting at a mark with his bow and
arrows, until he became tired, and started to build a fish
trap in the water. While he was piling up the stones in two
long walls a man came and stood on the bank and asked
him what he was doing. The boy told him, and the man
said, "Well, that's pretty hard work and you ought to rest a
while. Come and take a walk up the river."

The boy said, "No"; that he was going home to dinner soon.

"Come right up to my house," said the stranger, and I'll
give you a good dinner there and bring you home again in
the morning."

So the boy went with him up the river until they came to a
house, when they went in, and the man's wife and the other

people there were very glad to see him, and gave him a fine
dinner, and were very kind to him. While they were eating
a man that the boy knew very well came in and spoke to
him, so that he felt quite at home.

After dinner he played with the other children and slept
there that night, and in the morning, after breakfast, the
man got ready to take him home. They went down a path
that had a cornfield on one side and a peach orchard fenced
in on the other, until they came to another trail, and the man
said, "Go along this trail across that ridge and you will
come to the river road that will bring you straight to your
home, and now I'll go back to the house."

So the man went back to the house and the boy went on
along the trail, but when he had gone a little way he looked
back, and there was no cornfield or orchard or fence or
house; nothing but trees on the mountain side.

He thought it very queer, but somehow he was not
frightened, and went on until he came to the river trail in
sight of his home. There were a great many people standing
about talking, and when they saw him they ran toward him
shouting, "Here he is! He is not drowned or killed in the
mountains!" They told him they had been hunting him ever
since yesterday noon, and asked him where he had been.

"A man took me over to his house just across the ridge, and
I had a fine dinner and a good time with the children," said
the boy, "I thought Udsi'skalä here"--that was the name of
the man he had seen at dinner--"would tell you where I
was."

But Udsi'skalä said, "I haven't seen you. I was out all day in
my canoe hunting you. It was one of the Nûñnë'hï that
made himself look like me."

Then his mother said, "You say you had dinner there?"

"Yes, and I had plenty, too," said the boy; but his mother answered, "There is no house there--only trees and rocks--but we hear a drum sometimes in the big bald above. The people you saw were the Nûñnë'hï."

Once four Nûñnë'hï women came, to a dance at Nottely town, and danced half the night with the young men there, and nobody knew that they were Nûñnë'hï, but thought them visitors from another settlement.

About midnight they left to go home, and some men who had come out from the townhouse to cool off watched to see which way they went. They saw the women go down the trail to the river ford, but just as they came to the water they disappeared, although it was a plain trail, with no place where they could hide.

Then the watchers knew they were Nûñnë'hï women. Several men saw this happen, and one of them was Wafford's father-in-law, who was known for an honest man. At another time a man named Burnt-tobacco was crossing over the ridge from Nottely to Hemptown in Georgia and heard a drum and the songs of dancers in the hills on one side of the trail.

He rode over to see who could be dancing in such a place, but when he reached the spot the drum and the songs were behind him, and he was so frightened that he hurried back to the trail and rode all the way to Hemptown as hard as he could to tell the story. He was a truthful man, and they believed what he said.

There must have been a good many of the Nûñnë'hï living in that neighborhood, because the drumming wits often

heard in the high balds almost up to the time of the
Removal.

On a small upper branch of Nottely, running nearly due
north from Blood maintain, there was also a hole, like a
small well or chimney, in the ground, from which there
came up a warm vapor that heated all the air around. People
said that this was because the Nûñnë'hï had a townhouse
and a fire under the mountain. Sometimes in cold weather
hunters would stop there to warm the selves, but they were
afraid to stay long. This was more than sixty years ago, but
the hole is probably there yet.

Close to the old trading path from South Carolina up to the
Cherokee Nation, somewhere near the head of Tugaloo,
there was formerly a noted circular depression about the
size of a townhouse, and waist deep. Inside it was always
clean as though swept by unknown hands. Passing traders
would throw logs and rocks into it, but would always, on
their return, find them thrown far out from the hole. The
Indians said it was a Nunne'hi townhouse, and never liked
to go near the place or even to talk about it, until at last
some logs thrown in by the traders were allowed to remain
there, and then they concluded that the Nunne'hi, annoyed
by the persecution of the white men, had abandoned their
townhouse forever.

There is another race of spirits, the Yûñwï Tsunsdï, or
"Little People," who live in rock eaves on the mountain
side. They are little fellows, hardly reaching up to a man's
knee, but well shaped and handsome, with long hair falling
almost to the ground. They are great wonder workers and
are very fond of music, spending half their time drumming
and dancing.

They are helpful and kind-hearted, and often when people

have been lost in the mountains, especially children who have strayed away from their parents, the Yûñwĭ Tsunsdĭ' have found them and taken care of -them and brought them back to their homes. Sometimes their drum is heard in lonely places in the mountains, but it is not safe to follow it, because the Little

People do not like to be disturbed at home, and they throw a spell over the stranger so that he is bewildered and loses his way, and even if he does at last get back to the settlement he is like one dazed ever after.

Sometimes, also, they come near a house at night and the people inside hear them talking, but they must not go out, and in the morning they find the corn gathered or the field cleared as if a whole force of men had been at work. If anyone should go out to watch, he would die. When a hunter finds anything in the woods, such as a knife or a trinket, he must say, "Little People, I want to take this," because it may belong to them, and if he does not ask their permission they will throw stones at him as he goes home.

Once a hunter in winter found tracks in the snow like the tracks of little children. He wondered how they could have come there and followed them until they led him to a cave, which was full of Little People, young and old, men, women, and children. They brought him in and were kind to him, and he was with them some time; but when he left they warned him that he must not tell or he would die.

He went back to the settlement and his friends were all anxious to know where he had been. For a long time he refused to say, until at last he could not hold out any longer, but told the story, and in a few days he died. Only a few years ago two hunters from Raventown, going behind the high fall near the head of Oconaluftee on the East Cherokee reservation, found there a cave with fresh footprints of the Little People all over the floor.

During the smallpox among the East Cherokee just after the war one sick man wandered off, and his friends searched, but could not find him. After several weeks he came back and said that the Little People had found him and taken him to one of their eaves and tended him until he was cured.

About twenty-five years ago a man named Tsantäwû' was lost in the mountains on the head of Oconaluftee. It was winter time and very cold and his friends thought he must be dead, but after sixteen days he came back and said that the Little People had found him and taken him to their cave, where he had been well treated, and given plenty of everything to eat except bread. This was in large loaves, but when he took them in his hand to eat they seemed to shrink into small cakes so light and crumbly that though he might eat all day he would not be satisfied.

After he was well rested they had brought him a part of the way home until they came to a small creek, about knee deep, when they told him to wade across to reach the main trail on the other side. He waded across and turned to look back, but the Little People were gone and the creek was a deep river. When he reached home his legs were frozen to the knees and he lived only a few days.

Once the Yûñwï Tsunsdï' had been very kind to the people of a certain settlement, helping them at night with their work and taking good care of any lost children, until something happened to offend them and they made up their minds to leave the neighborhood. Those who were watching at the time saw the whole company of Little People come down to the ford of the river and cross over and disappear into the mouth of a large cave on the other side. They were never heard of near the settlement again.

There are other fairies, the Yûñwï Amaï'yïnë'hï, or Water-
dwellers, who live in the water, and fishermen pray to them
for help. Other friendly spirits live in people's houses,
although no one can see them, and so long as they are there
to protect the house no witch can come near to do mischief.

Tsäwa'sï and Tsäga'sï are the names of two small fairies,
who are mischievous enough, but yet often help the hunter
who prays to them. Tsäwa'sï, or Tsäwa'sï Usdï'ga (Little
Tsäwa'sï), is a tiny fellow, very handsome, with long hair
falling down to his feet, who lives in grassy patches on the
hillsides and has great power over the game.

To the deer hunter who prays to him he gives skill to slip
up on the deer through the long grass without being seen.
Tsäga'sï is another of the spirits invoked by the hunter and
is very helpful, but when someone trips and falls, we know
that it is Tsäga'sï who has caused it. There are several other
of these fairies with names, all good-natured, but more or
less tricky.

Then there is De'tsätä. De'tsätä was once a boy who ran
away to the woods to avoid a scratching and tries to keep
himself invisible ever since. He is a handsome little fellow
and spends his whole time hunting birds with blowgun and
arrow. He has a great many children who are all just like
him and have the same name. When a flock of birds flies
up suddenly as if frightened it is because De'tsätä is chasing
them.

He is mischievous and sometimes hides an arrow from the
bird hunter, who may have shot it off into a perfectly clear
space, but looks and looks without finding it. Then the
hunter says, "De'tsätä, you have my arrow, and if you don't

give it up I'll scratch you," and when he looks again he finds it.

There is one spirit that goes about at night with a light. The Cherokee call it Atsil'dihye'gï, "The Fire-carrier," and they are all afraid of it, because they think it dangerous, although they do not know much about it. They do not even know exactly what it looks like, because they are afraid to stop when they see it. It may be a witch instead of a spirit.

Wafford's mother saw the "Fire-carrier" once when she was a young woman, as she was coming home at night from a trading post in South Carolina. It seemed to be following her from behind, and. she was frightened and whipped up her horse until she got away from it and never saw it again.

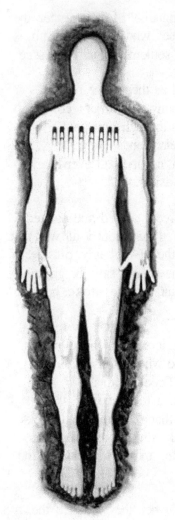

The Spirit Defenders of Nikwasi'

Cherokee

Long ago a powerful unknown tribe invaded the country from the southeast, killing people and destroying settlements wherever they went. No leader could stand against them, and in a little while they had wasted all the lower settlements and advanced into the mountains.

No leader could stand against them, and in a little while they had wasted all the lower settlements and advanced into the mountains.

The warriors of the old town of Nikwasi', on the head of Little Tennessee, gathered their wives and children into the townhouse and kept scouts constantly on the lookout for the presence of danger. One morning just before daybreak the spies saw the enemy approaching and at once gave the alarm.

The Nikwasi' men seized their arms and rushed out to meet the attack, but after a long, hard fight they found themselves overpowered and began to retreat, when suddenly a stranger stood among them and shouted to the chief to call off his men and he himself would drive back the enemy. From the dress and language of the stranger the Nikwasi' people thought him a chief who had come with reinforcements from the Overhill settlements in Tennessee.

They fell back along the trail, and as they came near the townhouse they saw a great company of warriors coming out from the side of the mound as through an open doorway. Then they knew that their friends were the Nûññë'hï, the Immortals, although no one had ever heard before that they lived under Nikwasi' mound.

The Nûññë'hï poured out by hundreds, armed and painted for the fight, and the most curious thing about it all was that they became invisible as soon as they were fairly outside of the settlement, so that although the enemy saw the glancing arrow or the rushing tomahawk, and felt the stroke, he could not see who sent it.

Before such invisible foes the invaders soon had to retreat, going first south along the ridge to where joins the main ridge which separates the French Broad from the Tuckasegee, and then turning with it to the northeast. As they retreated they tried to shield themselves behind rocks and trees, but the Nûññë'hï arrows went around the rocks and killed them from the other side, and they could find no hiding place.

All along the ridge they fell, until when they reached the head of Tuckasegee not more than half a dozen were left alive, and in despair they sat down and cried out for mercy. Ever since then the Cherokee have called the place Dayûlsûñ'yï, "Where they cried."

Then the Nûññë'hï chief told them they had deserved their punishment for attacking a peaceful tribe, and he spared their lives and told them to go home and take the news to their people. This was the Indian custom, always to spare a few to carry back the news of defeat. They went home toward the north and the Nûñnë'hï went back to the mound.

And they are still there, because, in the last war, when a strong party of Federal troops came to surprise a handful of Confederates posted there they saw so many soldiers guarding the town that they were afraid and went away without making an attack.

Blood Cot Boy
A Blackfoot Legend

Once there was an old man and woman whose three daughters married a young man. The old people lived in a lodge by themselves.

The young man was supposed to hunt buffalo, and feed them all. Early in the morning the young man invited his father-in-law to go out with him to kill buffalo. The old man was then directed to drive the buffalo through a gap where the young man stationed himself to kill them as they went by. As soon as the buffalo were killed, the young man requested his father-in-law to go home.

He said, "You are old. You need not stay here. Your daughters can bring you some meat." Now the young man lied to his father-in-law; for when the meat was brought to his lodge, he ordered his wives not to give meat to the old folks. Yet one of the daughters took pity on her parents, and stole meat for them. The way in which she did this was to take a piece of meat in her robe, and as she went for water drop it in front of her father's lodge.

Now every morning the young man invited his father-in-law to hunt buffalo; and, as before, sent him away and refused to permit his daughters to furnish meat for the old people. On the fourth day, as the old man was returning, he saw a clot of blood in the trail, and said to himself, "Here at least is something from which we can make soup."

In order that he might not be seen by his son-in-law, he stumbled, and spilt the arrows out of his quiver. Now, as he picked up the arrows, he put the clot of blood into the quiver. Just then the young man came up and demanded to know what it was he picked up. The old man explained that he had just stumbled, and was picking up his arrows.

So the old man took the clot of blood home and requested his wife to make blood-soup. When the pot began to boil, the old woman heard a child crying. She looked all around, but saw nothing. Then she heard it again. This time it seemed to be in the pot. She looked in quickly, and saw a boy baby: so she lifted the pot from the fire, took the baby out and wrapped it up.

Now the young man, sitting in his lodge, heard a baby crying, and said, "Well, the old woman must have a baby." Then he sent his oldest wife over to see the old woman's baby, saying, "If it is a boy, I will kill it." The woman came into look at the baby, but the old woman told her it was a girl. When the young man heard this, he did not believe it.

So he sent each wife in turn; but they all came back with the same report. Now the young man was greatly pleased, because he could look forward to another wife. So he sent over some old bones, that soup might be made for the baby. Now, all this happened in the morning.

That night the baby spoke to the old man, saying, "You take me up and hold me against each lodge-pole in succession." So the old man took up the baby, and, beginning at the door, went around in the direction of the sun, and each time that he touched a pole the baby became larger. When halfway around, the baby was so heavy that the old man could hold him no longer. So he put the baby down in the middle of the lodge, and, taking hold of his head, moved it toward each of the poles in succession, and, when the last pole was reached, the baby had become a very fine young man.

Then this young man went out, got some black flint [obsidian] and, when he got to the lodge, he said to the old man, "I am the Smoking-Star. I came down to help you. When I have done this, I shall return."

Now, when morning came, Blood-Clot (the name his father gave him) arose and took his father out to hunt. They had not gone very far when they killed a scabby cow. Then Blood-Clot lay down behind the cow and requested his father to wait until the son-in-law came to join him. He also requested that he stand his ground and talk back to the son-in-law.

Now, at the usual time in the morning, the son-in-law called at the lodge of the old man, but was told that he had gone out to hunt. This made him very angry, and he struck at the old woman, saying, "I have a notion to kill you." So the son-in-law went out.

Now Blood-Clot had directed his father to be eating a kidney when the son-in-law approached. When the son-in-law came up and saw all this, he was very angry. He said to the old man, "Now you shall die for all this."

"Well," said the old man, "you must die too, for all that you have done."

Then the son in-law began to shoot arrows at the old man, and the latter becoming frightened called on Blood-Clot for help. Then Blood-Clot sprang up and upbraided the son-in-law for his cruelty. "Oh," said the son-in-law, "I was just fooling." At this Blood-Clot shot the son-in-law through and through.

Then Blood-Clot said to his father, "We will leave this meat here: it is not good. Your son-in-law's house is full of dried meat. Which one of your daughters helped you?"

The old man told him that it was the youngest.

Then Blood-Clot went to the lodge, killed the two older women, brought up the body of the son-in-law, and burned them together. Then he requested the younger daughter to take care of her old parents, to be kind to them, etc. "Now," said Blood-Clot, "I shall go to visit the other Indians."

So he started out, and finally came to a camp. He went into the lodge of some old women, who were very much surprised to see such a fine young man. They said, "Why do you come here among such old women as we? Why don't you go where there are young people?"

"Well," said Blood-Clot, "give me some dried meat." Then the old women gave him some meat, but no fat. "Well," said Blood-Clot, "you did not give me the fat to eat with my dried meat."

"Hush!" said the old women. "You must not speak so loud. There are bears here that take all the fat and give us the lean, and they will kill you, if they hear you."

"Well," said Blood-Clot, "I will go out to-morrow, do some butchering, and get some fat." Then he went out through the camp, telling all the people to make ready in the morning, for he intended to drive the buffalo over [the drive].

Now there were some bears who ruled over this camp. They lived in a bear-lodge [painted lodge], and were very cruel. When Blood-Clot had driven the buffalo over, he noticed among them a scabby cow. He said, "I shall save this for the old women."

Then the people laughed, and said, "Do you mean to save that poor old beast? It is too poor to have fat." However, when it was cut open it was found to be very fat. Now, when the bears heard the buffalo go over the drive, they as usual sent out two bears to cut off the best meat, especially all the fat; but Blood-Clot had already butchered the buffalo, putting the fat upon sticks. He hid it as the bears came up.

Also he had heated some stones in a fire. When they told him what they wanted, he ordered them to go back. Now the bears were very angry, and the chief bear and his wife came up to fight, but Blood-Clot killed them by throwing hot stones down their throats.

Then he went down to the lodge of the bears and killed all, except one female who was about to become a mother. She pleaded so pitifully for her life, that he spared her. If he had not done this, there would have been no more bears in the world.

The lodge of the bears was filled with dried meat and other property. Also all the young women of the camp were confined there. Blood-Clot gave all the property to the old women, and set free all the young women. The bears' lodge he gave to the old women. It was a bear painted lodge.

"Now," said Blood-Clot, "I must go on my travels."

He came to a camp and entered the lodge of some old women. When these women saw what a fine young man he was, they said, "Why do you come here, among such old women? Why do you not go where there are younger people?"

"Well," said he, "give me some meat." The old women gave him some dried meat, but no fat.

Then he said, "Why do you not give me some fat with my meat?"

"Hush!" said the women, "you must not speak so loud. There is a snake- lodge [painted lodge] here, and the snakes take everything. They leave no fat for the people."

"Well," said Blood-Clot, "I will go over to the snake-lodge to eat."

"No, you must not do that," said the old women. "It is dangerous. They will surely kill you."

"Well," said he, "I must have some fat with my meat, even if they do kill me."

Then he entered the snake-lodge. He had his white rock knife ready. Now the snake, who was the head man in this lodge, had one horn on his head. He was lying with his head in the lap of a beautiful woman. He was asleep. By the fire was a bowl of berry-soup ready for the snake when he should wake. Blood-Clot seized the bowl and drank the soup.

Then the women warned him in whispers, "You must go
away: you must not stay here." But he said, "I want to
smoke." So he took out his knife and cut off the head of the
snake, saying as he did so, "Wake up! light a pipe! I want
to smoke."

Then with his knife he began to kill all the snakes. At last
there was one snake who was about to become a mother,
and she pleaded so pitifully for her life that she was
allowed to go. From her descended all the snakes that are in
the world.

Now the lodge of the snakes was filled up with dried meat
of every kind, fat, etc. Blood-Clot turned all this over to the
people, the lodge and everything it contained. Then he said,
"I must go away and visit other people."

So he started out. Some old women advised him to keep on
the south side of the road, because it was dangerous the
other way. But Blood-Clot paid no attention to their
warning. As he was going along, a great windstorm struck
him and at last carried him into the mouth of a great fish.

This was a sucker-fish and the wind was its sucking. When
he got into the stomach of the fish, he saw a great many
people. Many of them were dead, but some were still alive.
He said to the people, "Ah, there must be a heart
somewhere here. We will have a dance."

So he painted his face white, his eyes and mouth with black
circles, and tied a white rock knife on his head, so that the
point stuck up. Some rattles made of hoofs were also
brought. Then the people started in to dance. For a while
Blood-Clot sat making wing-motions with his hands, and
singing songs. Then he stood up and danced, jumping up
and down until the knife on his head struck the heart. Then

he cut the heart down. Next he cut through between the ribs of the fish, and let all the people out.

Again Blood-Clot said he must go on his travels. Before starting, the people warned him, saying that after a while he would see a woman who was always challenging people to wrestle with her, but that he must not speak to her. He gave no heed to what they said, and, after he had gone a little way, he saw a woman who called him to come over. "No," said Blood-Clot. "I am in a hurry."

However, at the fourth time the woman asked him to come over, he said, "Yes, but you must wait a little while, for I am tired. I wish to rest. When I have rested, I will come over and wrestle with you."

Now, while he was resting, he saw many large knives sticking up from the ground almost hidden by straw. Then he knew that the woman killed the people she wrestled with by throwing them down on the knives. When he was rested, he went over.

The woman asked him to stand up in the place where he had seen the knives; but he said, "No, I am not quite ready. Let us play a little, before we begin." So he began to play with the woman, but quickly caught hold of her, threw her upon the knives, and cut her in two.

Blood-Clot took up his travels again, and after a while came to a camp where there were some old women. The old women told him that a little farther on he would come to a woman with a swing, but on no account must he ride with her.

After a time he came to a place where he saw a swing on the bank of a swift stream. There was a woman swinging on it. He watched her a while, and saw that she killed people by swinging them out and dropping them into the water. When he found this out, he came up to the woman. "You have a swing here; let me see you swing," he said.

"No," said the woman, "I want to see you swing."

"Well," said Blood-Clot, "but you must swing first"

"Well,'" said the woman, "Now I shall swing. Watch me. Then I shall see you do it." So the woman swung out over the stream. As she did this, he saw how it worked. Then he said to the woman, "You swing again while I am getting ready"; but as the woman swung out this time, he cut the vine and let her drop into the water.

This happened on Cut Bank Creek.

"Now," said Blood-Clot, "I have rid the world of all the monsters, I will go back to my old father and mother." So he climbed a high ridge, and returned to the lodge of the old couple.

One day he said to them, "I shall go back to the place from whence I came. If you find that I have been killed, you must not be sorry, for then I shall go up into the sky and become the Smoking-Star."

Then he went on and on, until he was killed by some Crow Indians on the war- path. His body was never found; but the moment he was killed, the Smoking- Star appeared in the sky, where we see it now.